HEALTHY FOOD, HEALTHY YOU

delicious recipes to help you watch your weight

Adam Palmer

This is a Parragon Publishing Book
This edition published in 2005

Parragon Publishing
Queen Street House
4 Queen Street
Bath
BA1 1HE
United Kingdom

Created and produced by
The Bridgewater Book Company Ltd.

Parragon would like to thank Karen Thomas (photographer),
Valerie Berry (home economist), Breda Bradshaw (home economist),
and Charlie Parker (marketing nutritionist).

ISBN: 1-40544-759-1

Printed in China

NOTES

This symbol means the recipe is suitable for vegetarians.

This book uses imperial, metric, or US cup measurements. Follow the same
unit of measurement throughout; do not mix imperial and metric.

All spoon measurements are level unless otherwise specified.

Unless otherwise stated, milk is assumed to be full fat, eggs and individual
vegetables are medium, and pepper is freshly ground black pepper.

Recipes using raw or very lightly cooked eggs should be avoided by infants, the elderly,
pregnant women, convalescents, and anyone suffering from an illness. Pregnant and
breastfeeding women are advised to avoid eating peanuts and peanut products.

The times given are an approximate guide only. Preparation times differ according
to the techniques used by different people and the cooking times may also vary from those given.
Optional ingredients, variations, or serving suggestions have not been included in the calculations.

DISCLAIMER

*Before following any of the advice given in this book we recommend that you first check with your doctor.
Pregnant women, women planning to become pregnant, children, diabetics, or people with other medical
conditions should always check with their doctor or health care professional before embarking on any type
of diet. This book is not intended as a substitute for your doctor's or dietician's advice and support, but
should complement the advice they give you. The accuracy of the nutritional information (calorie and fat)
given for each recipe is dependent on following the recipe instructions.*

CONTENTS

introduction

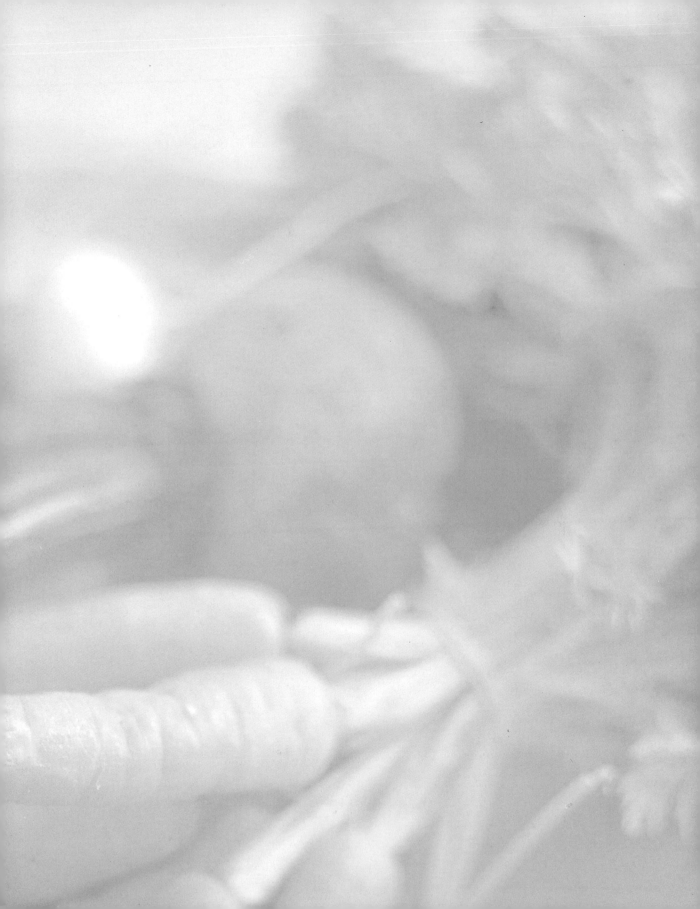

EAT YOURSELF HEALTHY

Healthy eating and weight loss do not rely simply on eating less food. A fitter, trimmer body requires certain changes in the way we prepare and cook our everyday food and when we eat it. There are hundreds of different diet plans for us to try—some of which are specific to one or two particular food groups and do not concentrate on adopting a varied and balanced approach to healthy eating. Food plays an important role in our well-being and with the hectic pace of modern life it is often much easier to skip meals and grab food "on the hoof" and snack throughout the day on highly processed foods which depend too much on fat, salt, and sugar for any flavor—all which we now know to be particularly detrimental, not only to our waistlines but also to our long-term health if consumed in quantity. The recipes in *Healthy Food, Healthy You* serve to demonstrate how you can lighten up your cooking by using less fat, salt, and sugar and instead draw on the natural flavors in foods, without any compromise on taste.

The use of vegetable oil sprays, cooking with nonstick cookware, and using silicone sheets on your roasting trays enables you to brown and caramelize meats, fish, and vegetables in the oven or under the broiler without having to use excessive amounts of added fat. Foods naturally contain salt so you should not add extra salt during cooking

but find alternative ways of boosting flavor. The recipes in this book include no added salt, relying instead on the additions of fresh herbs, spices, and citrus juice to enhance the taste experience of the finished dish.

What could be better than a homecooked meal prepared for your family and friends with the added advantage of being less than 3% fat, calorie-controlled, and low in salt and sugar?

We hope that the recipes will not only change your waistline but also the way you cook and enjoy your food.

Happy healthy cooking!

Adam Palmer

Adam Palmer, one of the UK's top chefs, is renowned for his healthy and innovative cuisine. He has developed the delicious recipes you will enjoy in this book. A former Executive Chef at Champney's Health Resort, Adam is a pioneer of delicious alternatives to outdated dietary practises. He is the author of two other cookery titles, has created recipes for many leading magazines in the USA, Europe, and the UK, and is a regular guest on TV cookery shows.

THE 3 MAIN REASONS THAT DIETS FAIL

Setting unrealistic goals—if you set unrealistic goals you're more likely to become disheartened and give up. Aim for a slow but steady weight loss of 1–2 lb (0.5–1 kg) a week. If you lose too much weight too quickly there's a danger of losing lean muscle tissue as well as fat.

Following the wrong sort of diet—however tempting they may seem, crash diets just don't work. Although you may lose weight initially, you'll find you'll end up putting on not just the weight you originally lost but more.

Not eating enough—a mistake people often make is to reduce their calorie intake too heavily. Overly strict diets are difficult to stick to in the long run, they're not necessary, and they're not healthy. If you restrict your calories too severely the chances are you'll end up missing out on important nutrients.

HOW TO USE THIS COOKBOOK

Losing weight isn't always easy, but the benefits are enormous—you'll feel fitter and more confident, you'll have more energy, and you'll be healthier. The good news is that losing weight doesn't mean having to say goodbye to your favorite foods: in fact, it's important to include the foods you enjoy eating. A diet which leaves you feeling deprived, unhappy, and dissatisfied is a diet that's very quickly going to be abandoned.

With increasing pressure on our daily schedule, many of us are tempted to skip meals. Don't! You're more likely to be tempted by a snack, and at your next meal you may overeat to compensate. Remember, too, that even when time is pressing, there are many simple meals that are quick and easy to make.

On a diet, your aim should be to achieve gradual but steady and sustained weight loss. This means following a nutritionally balanced eating plan, with a target intake for women of around 1400 calories a day and for men of around 2000 calories a day.

Following a diet can be very boring if you have to eat the same foods day after day. This book offers you a range of mouthwatering recipes, from breakfasts and quick lunches to entrées and even desserts. After all, you're not going to stick to a diet if you don't let yourself have a treat.

Breakfast   Lunch

Main meal   Dessert

Calorie-counting can often be a case of either guesswork or complicated calculations. The recipes in this book are intended to do the hard work for you; each recipe comes with a nutritional breakdown of the calorie, total fat, and saturated fat content.

HEALTHY EATING
A BALANCED APPROACH TO HEALTHY EATING

The food we eat can have an important and lasting effect on our health. The body needs over 40 different nutrients to stay healthy. Some, such as carbohydrates, proteins, and fats, are required in relatively large quantities, while others, such as vitamins, minerals, and trace elements, are required in minute amounts but are no less essential for health.

The best way to ensure that we get the full range of nutrients our bodies need is to eat a varied diet containing foods from each of the 5 major food groups. The secret to healthy eating and managing your weight is to get the balance right.

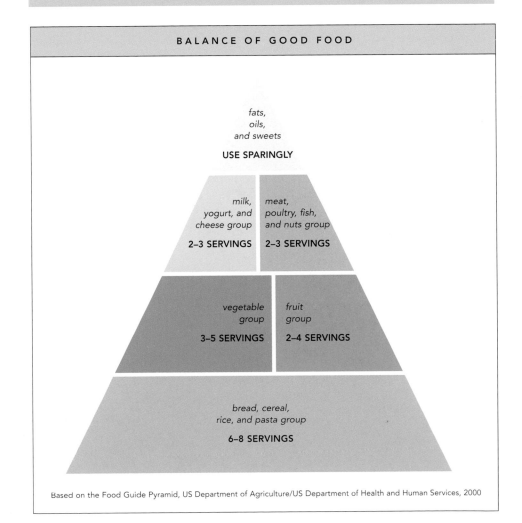

BALANCE OF GOOD FOOD

fats,
oils,
and sweets

USE SPARINGLY

milk,
yogurt, and
cheese group

2–3 SERVINGS

meat,
poultry, fish,
and nuts group

2–3 SERVINGS

vegetable
group

3–5 SERVINGS

fruit
group

2–4 SERVINGS

bread, cereal,
rice, and pasta group

6–8 SERVINGS

Based on the Food Guide Pyramid, US Department of Agriculture/US Department of Health and Human Services, 2000

GRAINS
(E.G. BREAD, RICE, PASTA, NOODLES, BREAKFAST CEREALS) —KNOWN AS CARBOHYDRATES

Foods from this group should provide 45–65% of your calories each day. These foods provide carbohydrates (starch and dietary fiber), protein, vitamins, and minerals, which are all important for good health.

Choose fiber-rich complex carbohydrates such as whole grain foods—they promote proper bowel function and will help you to feel full with few calories.

Contrary to what many people believe, foods from this group are not fattening in themselves, becoming highly calorific only when they are eaten with lots of fat (such as a rich, creamy sauce with pasta, sautéed potatoes, or bread that has been spread thickly with butter).

• Depending on your appetite and calorie requirement, aim to eat between 6 and 8 servings from this group each day.

1 serving equals:
1 cup breakfast cereal
1 slice bread
½ cup cooked rice
½ cup cooked pasta

FRUIT AND VEGETABLES

It's no coincidence that people from Mediterranean countries, who eat almost twice the amount of fruit and vegetables we do, live longer and remain healthier. Fruit and vegetables provide vitamins and minerals, dietary fiber, and other important substances.

The Food Guide Pyramid recommends that we should all aim to eat 2–4 servings of fruit and 3–5 servings of vegetables a day. This has been proved to help prevent a number of diseases, including heart disease and several forms of cancer.

Apart from being excellent providers of vitamins and minerals, most fruit and vegetables are fat-free and wonderfully low in calories. Make the most of them and look out for new recipes and ideas for cooking them—try poaching, baking, or broiling fruits as an alternative to eating them raw.

- Aim to eat at least 2 servings of fruit and 3 servings of vegetables a day.
- Adopt a rainbow approach—different colored fruit and vegetables provide different vitamins and minerals.
- Frozen, canned, and dried fruits and vegetables, as well as juices, are all useful in helping you reach your daily target.

1 serving equals 3 oz (85 g) of fruit or vegetables, a total of 15 oz (425 g) per day:

Fresh

Frozen

Dried

Canned

1 small glass (⅔ cup) unsweetened fruit juice

1 slice melon or pineapple

1 apple, orange, peach, or pear

¾ cup frozen peas, corn, or berries

1 tbsp dried fruit e.g. raisins

3 tbsp fruit salad or canned fruit or vegetables

MILK AND DAIRY
(E.G. MILK, YOGURT, CHEESE)

Dairy products are an important source of calcium, essential for strong bones and teeth. Many people, especially teenage girls, fail to eat enough calcium to meet their recommended daily requirement—putting them at risk of the bone disease osteoporosis in later life.

Dairy foods also provide protein, vitamin A, phosphorus, vitamin D, and vitamin B_2. Foods in this group can be high in fat, particularly saturated fat—choose reduced-fat and lowfat alternatives such as skim and lowfat milk. Calcium is contained in the non-creamy portion of milk, so the calcium remains when the fat is removed to make reduced-fat products—in fact, pint for pint, skim milk contains slightly more calcium than whole milk. Remember that this group does not include butter, eggs, and cream.

- Aim to eat 2–3 servings from this group a day.
- Choose lowfat and reduced-fat varieties whenever possible.

1 serving equals:
1 cup milk
1 cup yogurt
1½ oz (40 g) natural cheese, such as Cheddar
2 oz (55 g) processed cheese, such as American

MEAT, FISH AND ALTERNATIVES (POULTRY, EGGS, BEANS AND PULSES, NUTS AND SEEDS)

Foods from this group provide protein, needed for the production of enzymes, antibodies, and hormones. In short, protein is the building block of the body. Foods in this group are also a good source of iron, needed by the blood to circulate oxygen around the body. Low iron stores in the body can cause tiredness, lethargy, and possibly anemia.

• Aim to eat 2–3 servings from this group a day.
• Meat should be lean with any visible fat removed before cooking, and the skin should be removed from poultry.
• Meat can be fresh, frozen, or part of a prepared meal, but limit your intake of high-fat processed meats, such as bacon and sausages.
• Aim to eat 1–2 servings of oil-rich fish, such as salmon or tuna, a week. They are rich in omega-3 fatty acids, and help to reduce the risk of heart disease.
• Vegetarians should eat a variety of different protein foods to ensure they get all the nutrients they need.

1 serving equals approximately:
2–3 oz (55–85 g) cooked lean meat, poultry, or fish*

*1 oz (30 g) of lean meat, poultry or fish is equal to:
½ cup of cooked dry beans,
½ cup of tofu,
1 egg, 2 tbsp of peanut butter,
or ⅓ cup of nuts

FOODS CONTAINING FATS AND SUGARS

Small amounts of fat are vital in our diet to provide essential fatty acids and to facilitate the absorption of fat-soluble vitamins, but a high-fat diet is known to increase the risk of heart disease, certain types of cancer, and obesity. A diet that is rich in saturated fats, found in foods such as fatty cuts of meat and meat products, full-fat dairy products, and butter and some types of margarine increases the levels of cholesterol in the blood.

Weight for weight, fat provides twice as many calories as carbohydrate or protein. There is also some evidence to suggest that calories eaten as fat are more likely to be laid down as body fat than calories from protein or carbohydrate. The good news is that these days low in fat doesn't have to mean low in taste. There are easy ways to trim the fat from your diet (see page 20) without giving up the foods you enjoy.

Sugar provides "empty" calories—calories that provide nothing else in the way of protein, fiber, vitamins, or minerals, and calories that most of us could do without. So it makes sense to cut down on it where you can. Sugar and sugary foods also increase the risk of tooth decay, especially when eaten between meals.

- Total fat should provide less than 30% of your total calories each day. For a woman eating 2000 calories a day, this amounts to about 2½ oz (70 g) of fat or less.
- Saturated fat should provide less than 10% of your total fat intake. For a woman eating 2000 calories a day, this amounts to about ¾ oz (20 g) of fat or less.
- Look at the nutritional labeling on food packaging to check the fat content of the food. Try to choose foods that are low in saturated fat.
- Avoid adding sugar to food.

DIETARY FIBER

Although it passes through our digestive tract unchanged, fiber is essential for a healthy digestive system.

Fiber can be divided into 2 groups: insoluble fiber and soluble fiber. Insoluble fiber is found mainly in wheat, whole-grain cereals, fruit and vegetables, and dried beans, peas, and lentils. It has the effect of holding or absorbing water, which helps to prevent constipation and diverticular disease. It also speeds up the rate at which waste material is passed through the body, and this is believed to play an important role in preventing colon cancer by reducing the length of time that cancer-causing toxins stay within the digestive system.

Soluble fiber, found in oats and oat bran, dried beans, peas, and lentils, and some fruits, can help to lower high blood cholesterol levels and slow down the absorption of sugar into the bloodstream.

The recommended daily intake of dietary fiber for men and women is 1–1¼ oz (25–35 g).

EASY WAYS TO INCREASE YOUR FIBER INTAKE:

• Choose a whole grain cereal such as oatmeal, granola, or bran flakes for breakfast. Pick one that provides 3 g of fiber or more per serving.
• Choose whole wheat, whole oat, or whole rye bread. Bread may be brown, but this doesn't necessarily mean that it is high in fiber—look for the words "whole grain" or "whole wheat" on the label.
• Eat more dried beans, peas, and lentils such as red kidney beans and chickpeas.
• Eat a minimum of 2 servings of fruit and 3 servings of vegetables a day.
• Eat dried fruit as snack between meals or add it to your breakfast cereal.
• Use brown rather than white rice, and whole wheat pasta.

SALT (SODIUM CHLORIDE)

Sodium plays a vital role in the body's fluid balance as well as being involved in muscle and nerve activity. Almost all of us, however, consume far more than is good for us. A high salt intake is believed to be a major factor in the development of high blood pressure, which increases the risk of stroke and heart disease.

- Experts recommend moderating your daily salt intake to no more than 2400 mg. This is only 1 teaspoon of salt, which is around half our current average intake. Healthy adults actually only need less than ¼ teaspoon of salt daily to meet their sodium requirement.
- Around 80% of the sodium in our diet comes from processed foods—1 small can of chicken soup, for instance, can contain over half the recommended daily amount.
- Train your taste buds to enjoy foods with less salt. Try using herbs and spices to enhance the flavor of food.
- Generally, foods that contain more than 500 mg sodium per serving are high in sodium. Foods that contain less than 100 mg sodium per serving are low in sodium. Always read the nutritional labeling on packaging.

WATER

Water is vital to good health. Unlike some other nutrients, the human body does not store water, so you need to drink a regular supply.

Some foods, particularly fruit and vegetables, contain quite a lot of water—a slice of watermelon, for instance, is 92% water and an apple 84%—and eating them can help replace some of the water lost by the body. We still need to drink around 8–10 glasses of fluid each day to prevent the body from becoming dehydrated.

Around 85% of our brain tissue is water—which explains why even mild dehydration can lead to problems such as headaches, lethargy, dizziness, and an inability to concentrate. Long-term dehydration can lead to digestive problems, kidney problems, and joint pain. Relying on thirst to tell you when you need to take a drink is not always a good idea—by the time you feel thirsty, your body is probably already mildly dehydrated.

- Drink at least 8–10 glasses (a glass is about 8 fl oz/225 ml) of fluid a day.
- Don't always rely on thirst as a sign that you need to take a drink.
- Eating plenty of fruit and vegetables will help increase your fluid intake.
- Take water breaks rather than coffee breaks at regular intervals during the day.
- Keeping a bottle of water on your desk at work will remind you to take a drink.
- To check to see you are drinking enough fluid, look at your urine—if you're drinking enough, it should be a light yellow color. Dark yellow urine is a sign that you're not drinking enough.
- Drink plenty of water before, during, and after taking exercise—especially if you are exercising in warm weather.

ALCOHOL

Alcohol is not forbidden on a diet, but it is worth remembering that for most of us willpower dissolves in alcohol! A glass of wine may be only 100 calories, but the trouble is that 1 glass easily leads to another, and after a couple of drinks it's easy to forget about your good intentions to eat healthily. If you drink alcohol, do so in moderation, which means no more than 1 serving per day for women and no more than 2 servings per day for men.

1 serving equals:
5 fl oz (150 ml) wine
12 fl oz (350 ml) regular beer
1½ fl oz (40 ml) spirits

8 STEPS TO A HEALTHY DIET

Enjoy your food

Eat a variety of different foods

Eat the right amount to achieve a healthy weight

Eat plenty of complex carbohydrates and fiber

Eat plenty of fruit and vegetables

Don't eat too many foods that contain a lot of fat

Don't have sugary foods and drinks too often

Drink alcohol in moderation

LOSING WEIGHT SAFELY

If you're trying to lose weight, you're not alone. In 1999, statistics showed that 61% of adults in the US were classified as overweight (BMI over 25—see page 19) or obese (BMI over 30). The number of obese people in the US has doubled in the last 2 decades. Many nutritionists believe that the reason for this alarming rise is due not to our eating more, but to our doing less. Modern technology and labor-saving devices mean that we're much less active than we used to be.

Our weight is a reflection of the balance between the energy (calories) we consume and the energy we use. Our energy intake is determined by the amount and type of food we eat. Our energy expenditure is determined by a combination of our resting metabolic rate and the amount of calories we burn in day-to-day activities.

The resting metabolic rate is the amount of energy our body needs during rest or sleep. This is similar to the fuel used by a car when the engine is idling but the car is stationary.

If our energy intake equals our energy expenditure, our body weight will remain the same, but if our intake exceeds our expenditure, the excess energy is stored in the body as fat (see below).

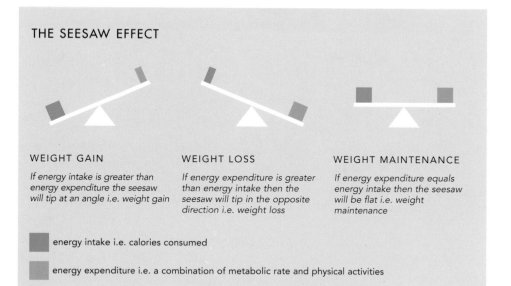

THE SEESAW EFFECT

WEIGHT GAIN

If energy intake is greater than energy expenditure the seesaw will tip at an angle i.e. weight gain

WEIGHT LOSS

If energy expenditure is greater than energy intake then the seesaw will tip in the opposite direction i.e. weight loss

WEIGHT MAINTENANCE

If energy expenditure equals energy intake then the seesaw will be flat i.e. weight maintenance

energy intake i.e. calories consumed

energy expenditure i.e. a combination of metabolic rate and physical activities

THE IDEAL RATE OF WEIGHT LOSS

Experts agree the best and safest way to lose weight is slowly and steadily—between 1–2 lb (0.5–1 kg) a week is the ideal rate. If you lose too much weight too quickly, there is a danger of losing lean muscle tissue as well as fat. Since our basal metabolic rate (the number of calories the body needs to function) is related to the amount of lean muscle tissue we have, it's a good idea to do whatever we can to preserve it.

HOW LOW SHOULD YOU GO?

The total number of calories we need to eat each day varies, depending on a number of factors, including age, weight, sex, activity levels, body composition, and metabolic rate. As a general guide, women need around 2000 calories a day and men need 2500. To lose 1 lb (0.5 kg) a week, you need to reduce your calorie intake by 500 calories a day. Diets that restrict calories too severely (fewer than 1200 calories a day) are not recommended.

HOW YOU SHAPE UP

Although most of us can get a pretty good idea of whether we need to lose weight or not just by looking in the mirror, you can get a more accurate assessment by calculating your Body Mass Index or waist circumference (see panel below).

HOW YOU SHAPE UP

BMI (Body Mass Index) =

$$\frac{\text{weight in pounds}}{(\text{height in inches}) \times (\text{height in inches})} \times 703$$

For example, a person who weighs 145 pounds and is 5 feet 8 inches tall has a BMI of 22.

$$\frac{145 \text{ pounds}}{(68 \text{ inches}) \times (68 \text{ inches})} \times 703 = 22$$

Below 18.5	*underweight*
18.5–24.9	*normal weight range*
25.0–29.9	*overweight*
Over 30	*obese*

(Source: Centers for Disease Control and Prevention, 2003)

WAIST CIRCUMFERENCE

Men
Waist circumference over 37 in (94 cm)
indicates a slight health risk

Waist circumference over 40 in (102 cm)
indicates a substantial health risk

Women
Waist circumference over 32 in (80 cm)
indicates a slight health risk

Waist circumference over 35 in (88 cm)
indicates a substantial health risk

TRIMMING THE FAT

Fat provides twice as many calories as either protein or carbohydrate, which is why the most effective way of reducing calories is to limit the amount of fat you use.

- Start with lowfat ingredients—white fish, shellfish, chicken, and lean meat are all good choices.
- Trim off visible fat from meat before cooking and remove the skin from poultry. Avoid red meat that has too much fat or marbling.
- Choose lowfat cooking techniques—poach, braise, steam, broil, or stir-fry. Marinades are a good way of adding extra flavor without fat.
- Invest in a good heavy-bottom nonstick pan and remember that oil expands once it gets hot—so when you're softening onions or vegetables you don't need to add as much as you might think. Use a vegetable or olive oil nonstick cooking spray for dishes that require light sautéing.
- You don't need fat to add flavor—use plenty of fresh herbs and spices in your cooking. Adding a squeeze of fresh lemon juice just before serving can give food a real flavor boost.
- Bulk out savory dishes by adding plenty of vegetables. They are low in calories and provide essential vitamins.
- Use reduced- and lowfat alternatives such as reduced-fat cheese, skim milk, and lowfat yogurts where available.
- To make gravies and sauces creamy, add yogurt or ricotta rather than cream. Stir in at the end of cooking to prevent curdling.
- Using cheese with a strong flavor, such as sharp Cheddar, Parmesan, or blue cheese, will mean that you need to add less.
- Don't be afraid to use high-fat foods such as cheese and bacon: you will need only small quantities to add a lot of flavor.
- 1 tablespoon of French dressing contains 97 calories and about 11 g (¼ oz) of fat. Use sparingly or choose a lowfat dressing.

ESSENTIAL TIPS FOR LOSING WEIGHT FOREVER

1 / **Recognize why you overeat**—before you reach for a chocolate bar or slice of cake, ask yourself if you're really hungry. Keep a food diary to help you identify danger times when you are more likely to overeat.

2 / **Believe you can do it**—a recent study found that people who believed they could lose weight and keep it off were more likely to succeed. Try to visualize the new, slimmer you and keep that image in your mind.

3 / Eat slowly and chew your food thoroughly—the brain takes 15 minutes to get the message that your stomach has had enough to eat. If you eat too quickly, your stomach fills up before your brain knows you are full, and you end up eating too much.

4 / Never skip meals or let yourself get overhungry. If you do, you'll be more tempted to snack and overeat at your next meal. Aim to eat 3 small to medium-size meals a day plus 2 or 3 small, healthy snacks.

5 / Always eat breakfast—if you skip breakfast, you're more likely to snack during the morning and overeat at lunch.

6 / Get fruity—fruit and vegetables are a dieter's best friend: they're low in calories and fat-free. Aim to eat at least 5 servings a day. Be adventurous and try something new. Look for recipes and ideas for new ways of cooking fruit or vegetables.

7 / Stack up with starches and fill up with fiber—choose fiber-rich varieties such as whole-wheat bread and whole-grain cereals whenever possible. These provide slow-release energy, which helps keep blood sugar levels stable.

8 / Be prepared—make sure your cupboards and freezer are full of healthy foods and have plenty of low-calorie snacks available.

9 / Don't feel that 1 bad day will ruin the whole diet—life is full of ups and downs, so if you do lapse on the odd bad day, be a little stricter with yourself the following day.

10 / Never go shopping on an empty stomach—always write a list and stick to it! Don't buy foods you know you won't be able to resist.

11 / Don't deny yourself the foods you enjoy—just eat them in moderation.

12 / Drink at least 8 glasses of water a day—it's easy to confuse thirst with hunger. When you think you're feeling hungry, try drinking a large glass of water first.

13 / Trim the fat—fat is a dieter's biggest enemy. Whenever possible, choose products that are low in fat.

14 / Make use of every opportunity you can to stay active—use the stairs instead of the elevator or escalator, get off the bus 1 stop early and walk the rest of the way home. Small changes all add up and can make a big difference.

HELPLINES / CONTACTS

American Dietetic Association
120 South Riverside Plaza, Suite 2000,
Chicago, IL 60606-6995
Tel: 800 877 1600
Website: www.eatright.org

American Society for Nutritional Sciences
9650 Rockville Pike, Bethesda, MD 20814-3990
Tel: 301 634 7985, 301 634 7892
Website: www.nutrition.org Email: jnutrition@asns.org

National Eating Disorders Association
603 Stewart Street, Suite 803, Seattle, WA 98101
Tel: 206 382 3587
Website: www.nationaleatingdisorders.org
Email: info@NationalEatingDisorders.org

American Obesity Association
1250 24th Street NW, Suite 300, Washington DC 20037
Tel: 202 776 7711
Website: www.obesity.org Email: executive@obesity.org

In many ways, breakfast is the most important meal of the day. It follows a considerable period of fasting, during which period your blood sugar levels drop, so this is a crucial time for refueling for the hours ahead.

Breakfasts

Potentially, breakfast is a great opportunity to start a healthy eating regime, as many nutritious, lowfat foods such as cereals, fruit, porridge, and yogurts are already commonly consumed in this meal. However, beware certain varieties of these products—they can in fact be high in salt, sugar and fat, so check the nutritional information on the label.

We are not at our most culinary creative first thing in the morning, so plan ahead the night before. Aim to eat about 20–25% of your daily calorie intake at breakfast, to keep you going right through until lunchtime without the need for a midmorning pit stop. Remember that you can add a lowfat yogurt or a slice of dry toast to any of the dishes in this chapter for the perfect meal to start the day.

Watermelon, orange, and ginger cocktail with granola

(V) | **prep** 20 minutes + 1 hour cooling/chilling | **cook** 15 minutes | **serves** 4

for the granola
1 tbsp rolled oats
½ tbsp sesame seeds
pinch of ground ginger
½ tbsp sunflower seeds
2 tsp freshly squeezed orange juice
1 tsp honey

for the fruit cocktail
10½ oz (300 g) seeded watermelon, cut into chunks
3½ oz (100 g) fresh orange segments
6 tbsp freshly squeezed orange juice
1 tsp finely grated orange zest
1 tsp peeled and finely sliced gingerroot
1 tsp honey
½ tsp arrowroot, blended with a little cold water

1. Preheat the oven to 350°F/180°C.
2. To make the granola, put all the dry ingredients into a bowl, then add the orange juice and honey and mix thoroughly. Spread out on a nonstick baking sheet and bake for 7–8 minutes. Remove from the oven, break up into pieces, then return to the oven for an additional 7–8 minutes. Remove from the oven and break up again. Let cool on the baking sheet. The mixture will become crunchy when cool.
3. To make the fruit cocktail, put the watermelon and orange segments into a bowl. Put the orange juice and zest, ginger, and honey into a small pan over medium heat and bring to a boil. Gradually stir in the arrowroot mixture and cook, stirring constantly, until thickened.
4. Pour the mixture over the fruit and let cool, cover, and let chill in the refrigerator.
5. Spoon the covered fruit into glasses and sprinkle over the granola.

COOK'S TIPS
• *This dish can be prepared in advance and assembled just before eating.*
• *The granola will keep well in an airtight container for several days and can be used with other fruit combinations.*

NUTRITION INFORMATION
per serving

calories	fat	sat fat
73	2 g	0.2 g

Mini butternut squash crêpes with plum tomatoes and prosciutto

prep 10 minutes | **cook** 40–55 minutes | **serves** 4

for the crêpes
4¾ oz (130 g), peeled weight, butternut squash
2¼ oz (60 g) 0% fat plain yogurt
1 tsp maple syrup
pinch of cayenne pepper
1 tsp canola or vegetable oil
pinch of baking powder
1 tbsp whole wheat flour
1 egg white, lightly beaten
canola or vegetable oil spray

for the filling
10½ oz (300 g) baby plum tomatoes
2 tbsp balsamic vinegar
1 tsp maple syrup
1 tsp finely chopped fresh thyme
4 thin slices prosciutto, all visible fat removed

1. Preheat the oven to 350°F/180°C.
2. To make the crêpes, halve the peeled butternut squash and scoop out the seeds. Cut the flesh into chunks and spread out on a nonstick baking sheet. Roast for 15–20 minutes, or until tender but not colored.
3. Using a hand-held electric blender, blend the squash with the yogurt, maple syrup, cayenne, oil, and baking powder in a large bowl until smooth, or use a food processor. Beat in the flour, then fold in the egg white.
4. Spray a nonstick skillet lightly with oil and heat until just smoking. Pour in a level 1 tbsp of the batter and cook until bubbles appear on the surface. Flip over and cook for an additional 1–2 minutes. Remove and keep warm. Repeat with the remaining batter. You will need 3 crêpes per serving.
5. Meanwhile, preheat the broiler to hot. Halve the tomatoes, place in a large bowl with the vinegar, maple syrup, and thyme, and gently mix. Transfer to a nonstick baking sheet and broil for 4 minutes. Add the prosciutto to the edges of the sheet and broil for 2 minutes, or until crispy.
6. To serve, layer the crêpes with the tomatoes and top with the prosciutto. Drizzle over the cooking juices.

NUTRITION INFORMATION

per serving

calories	fat	sat fat
93	4 g	0.7 g

Mango, lime, and lemongrass zinger

(V) | **prep** 10 minutes + 2 hours chilling | **serves** 4

⅓ cup freshly squeezed lime juice
1 oz (25 g) lemongrass, plus 2 extra stalks, peeled and halved, to garnish
1 small very ripe mango
3 cups low-calorie tonic water
8 ice cubes, to serve

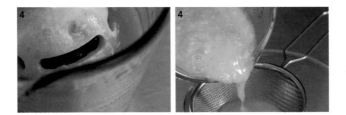

1. Pour the lime juice into a glass bowl.
2. Remove the outer brown part of the lemongrass and discard. Finely shred the remaining parts and add to the lime juice.
3. Cut lengthwise through the mango either side of the flat central seed. Cut away the flesh from around the seed and peel. Coarsely chop the flesh and add to the bowl.
4. Using a hand-held electric blender, blend until the mango is smooth, or use a food processor. Cover the bowl with plastic wrap and refrigerate for at least 2 hours before passing through a fine strainer.
5. Put a couple of ice cubes each into 4 glasses, divide the mango purée between the glasses, and top off with tonic water. Add a halved lemongrass stalk to each glass to use as a stirrer.

COOK'S TIP

• *Refrigerate the mango purée overnight before passing through a strainer to extract the maximum flavor from the lemongrass.*

NUTRITION INFORMATION

per serving

calories	fat	sat fat
23	0.1 g	0.0 g

Spiced whole wheat muffins
with marmalade and raspberry yogurt

Ⓥ | prep 15 minutes | cook 30 minutes | serves 6

canola or vegetable oil spray
scant 1 cup all-purpose flour
½ tsp baking powder
scant ½ cup whole wheat flour
½ tsp ground allspice
1 tbsp canola or vegetable oil
1 egg, lightly beaten
⅔ cup buttermilk
1 tsp grated orange zest
1 tbsp freshly squeezed orange juice
1 tsp low-sugar marmalade, for glazing

for the filling
generous ⅓ cup 0% fat strained plain yogurt
1 tsp low-sugar marmalade
½ tsp grated orange zest
scant ½ cup fresh raspberries

1. Preheat the oven to 325°F/160°C. Spray a six-hole muffin pan lightly with oil.
2. Sift the all-purpose flour with the baking powder into a large mixing bowl. Using a fork, stir in the whole wheat flour and allspice until thoroughly mixed.
3. Pour in the oil and rub into the flour mixture with your fingertips.
4. In a separate bowl, mix the egg, buttermilk, and orange zest and juice together, then pour into the center of the flour mixture and mix with a metal spoon, being careful not to overmix—the batter should look a little uneven and lumpy.
5. Spoon the batter into the prepared pan to come about three-quarters of the way up the sides of each hole. Bake in the oven for 30 minutes, or until golden brown and a skewer inserted into the center of a muffin comes out clean.
6. Remove from the oven and transfer to a wire rack. Brush with the marmalade and let cool.
7. For the filling, mix the yogurt with the marmalade and orange zest. Cut the warm muffins through the center and fill with the yogurt mixture and raspberries.

COOK'S TIP
• *These muffins are best served warm, about 30 minutes after removing from the oven, and will work well with low-sugar raspberry jelly instead of marmalade if you prefer.*

NUTRITION INFORMATION

per serving

calories	fat	sat fat
150	3.5 g	0.5 g

Soups and salads are a fantastic way of encouraging the whole family to enjoy a wide range of fruit and vegetables. For many years, nutritionists have encouraged us to eat more fruit and vegetables, and that advice is still very current. So five a day is here to stay.

Soups, salads, anc

When making soups and salads, be bold with flavors and textures. Remember, for instance, that a thick, puréed type of soup will always satisfy more than a thin, clear soup and that salads with contrasting textures and interesting tastes will be far more appetizing. So take a break from your routine lunchtime fare and substitute your usual sandwich for a vibrant, homemade soup, salad, or pasta dish. After all, variety is the spice of life.

light lunches

Golden bell pepper and yam soup

(V) | prep 20 minutes | cook 35 minutes | serves 4

2¾ oz (75 g), peeled weight, onion, finely chopped
2 garlic cloves, peeled and finely sliced
1¾ oz (50 g) leek (white part only), cut into ½-inch (1-cm) cubes
1¾ oz (50 g) celery, cut into ½-inch (1-cm) cubes
3¼ oz (90 g), peeled weight, potato, cut into ½-inch (1-cm) cubes
6¼ oz (180 g), peeled weight, yam, cut into ½-inch (1-cm) cubes
pinch of ground turmeric
pinch of ground mace
2 bay leaves
3½ cups vegetable stock
3¼ oz (90 g) seeded yellow bell pepper, roasted, peeled, and chopped
1 tbsp sugar
2 tsp lemon juice
flat bread, to serve

for the garnish
1 tsp canola or vegetable oil
1½ oz (40 g) cooked corn kernels
½ tsp habanero chili pepper sauce

1. Put the onion, garlic, leek, and celery into a large pan over high heat and cook, stirring constantly, for 5 minutes, or until softened but not colored. You will not need any oil as the steam and the continuous stirring will prevent the vegetables from sticking.
2. Add the potato, yam, turmeric, mace, bay leaves, and stock, stir well, and bring to a boil. Reduce the heat, cover, and let simmer for 20 minutes, or until all the vegetables are soft.
3. Meanwhile, in a separate pan, heat the oil, add the corn, and stir-fry until golden brown. Remove from the heat and stir in the chili sauce. Set aside for garnishing the soup.
4. Remove the bay leaves from the soup and discard. Stir in the roasted bell pepper, sugar, and lemon juice. Using a hand-held electric blender, blend the soup until smooth, or use a food processor.
5. Ladle into warmed soup bowls, sprinkle with the corn garnish, and serve, accompanied by flat bread.

NUTRITION INFORMATION
per serving

calories	fat	sat fat
93	1 g	0.1 g

Creamy lima bean, porcini, and tarragon soup

(V) | prep 15 minutes + 8 hours soaking | cook 1 hour 55 minutes | serves 4

2½ oz (70 g) leek (white part only), cut into ½-inch (1-cm) cubes
3½ oz (100g), peeled weight, onion, cut into ½-inch (1-cm) cubes
2½ oz (70 g) celery, cut into ½-inch (1-cm) cubes
1 garlic clove, peeled and crushed
2 bay leaves
5½ oz (150 g) fresh open-cap mushrooms, cut into ½-inch (1-cm) cubes,
    plus 2 tbsp diced to garnish
⅛ cup dried porcini mushrooms, soaked in ¼ cup hot water and drained
3 oz (85 g), peeled weight, potato, cut into ½-inch (1-cm) cubes
4 oz (115 g) canned lima beans, drained and rinsed under cold water
3 cups vegetable stock
1 tbsp chopped fresh tarragon, plus extra to garnish
½ cup skim milk

for the garnish
2 tsp lemon juice
1½ tsp sugar
pinch of pepper
3 tbsp 0% fat sour cream

1. Put the leek, onion, celery, and garlic into a large pan over high heat and cook, stirring constantly, for 5 minutes, or until softened but not colored. You will not need any oil as the steam and the continuous stirring will prevent the vegetables from sticking.
2. Add the bay leaves, mushrooms, potato, beans, stock, and tarragon, stir well, and bring to a boil. Reduce the heat, cover, and let simmer for 20 minutes, or until the vegetables are mushy.
3. Meanwhile, for the garnish, mix the lemon juice, sugar, and pepper together in a separate pan. Add the diced mushroom, cover, and cook over high heat for 4–5 minutes. Remove from the heat and let cool in the pan.
4. Remove the bay leaves from the soup and discard. Using a hand-held electric blender, blend the soup until smooth, or use a food processor. Stir in the milk. Pass through a medium strainer into a serving dish.
5. To serve, pour the mushroom garnish into the soup, sprinkle over a little tarragon, and add a swirl of sour cream.

NUTRITION INFORMATION

per serving

calories	fat	sat fat
97	0.8 g	0.1 g

Chickpea, saffron, and lemon chermoula soup

(V) | **prep** 25 minutes + 8 hours soaking | **cook** 2 hours 10 minutes | **serves** 6

1¾ oz (50 g) leek, cut into ½-inch (1-cm) cubes

3½ oz (100 g), peeled weight, onion, cut into ½-inch (1-cm) cubes

1¾ oz (50 g) celery, cut into ½-inch (1-cm) cubes

3 oz (85 g), peeled weight, carrot, cut into ½-inch (1-cm) cubes

2 cloves garlic, peeled and crushed

1 tbsp coriander seeds

4 oz (115 g) tomatoes

5 oz (140 g) canned chickpeas, drained and rinsed under cold water

1 litre (1¾ pints) vegetable stock

3½ oz (100 g), peeled weight, potato, cut into ½-inch (1-cm) cubes

2 bay leaves

pinch of saffron threads

2 lemons, halved, cut sides charred for 2–5 minutes in a hot nonstick skillet

for the chermoula

2 garlic cloves, peeled and finely sliced

½ red chili, finely chopped

1 tsp paprika

1 tsp ground cumin

1 tsp lemon juice

2 tsp white wine vinegar

4 tbsp finely chopped fresh flat-leaf parsley

4 tbsp finely chopped fresh cilantro leaves

1. Put the leek, onion, celery, carrot, and garlic into a large pan over high heat and cook, stirring constantly, for 5 minutes, or until softened but not colored. (You will not need any oil.) Add the coriander seeds and cook for an additional 2 minutes.

2. Add the tomatoes, chickpeas, stock, potato, bay leaves, and saffron, stir well, and bring to a boil. Reduce the heat, cover, and let simmer for 20 minutes, or until the vegetables are mushy.

3. To make the chermoula, pound the garlic with the spices, lemon juice, and vinegar to a smooth paste in a mortar with a pestle. Transfer to a pan, add the herbs, and gently warm for 5 minutes to infuse the flavors. Do not boil.

4. Remove the bay leaves, then blend the soup using a hand-held blender, or use a food processor. Pass through a medium strainer into warmed serving bowls. Top with the chermoula and serve with the charred lemons for squeezing over.

COOK'S TIP

• *Using the charred lemons for the seasoning gives a similar flavor to pickled lemons, which taste great but have a very high salt content.*

NUTRITION INFORMATION

per serving

calories	fat	sat fat
60	1 g	0.1 g

Gazpacho with crab, scallion, and sour cream

prep 15 minutes | **serves** 2

for the gazpacho
2½ oz (70 g) seeded red bell pepper, cut into ½-inch (1-cm) squares
1¾ oz (50 g) seeded green bell pepper, cut into ½-inch (1-cm) squares
2½ oz (70 g), peeled weight, onion, cut into ½-inch (1-cm) cubes
7 oz (200 g) tomatoes
3½ oz (100 g) cucumber
1 tbsp red wine vinegar
2 tbsp freshly squeezed orange juice
2 tbsp freshly squeezed lemon juice
1 garlic clove, peeled and finely sliced
pinch of paprika
pinch of cayenne pepper
pinch of freshly ground black pepper

for the garnish
⅛ cup 0% fat cream cheese
2 tbsp 15% fat sour cream
¼ oz (10 g) scallion, finely sliced
1 oz (25 g) cooked white crabmeat
2 tsp extra virgin olive oil

1. Put all the ingredients for the gazpacho into a large bowl. Using a hand-held electric blender, blend until smooth, or use a food processor.
2. To prepare the garnish, mix the cream cheese, sour cream, scallion, and crabmeat together in a small bowl. Cover and store in the refrigerator until ready to serve.
3. To serve, pour the soup into serving bowls, then top with the crabmeat mixture and drizzle over the oil.

NUTRITION INFORMATION

per serving

calories	fat	sat fat
142	6 g	2 g

41

Potato, herb, and smoked salmon gratin

prep 25 minutes + 20 minutes cooling | **cook** 50 minutes | **serves** 6

1¾ cups lowfat milk
3 whole cloves
2 bay leaves
1¾ oz (50 g), peeled weight, onion, sliced
3 oz (85 g) leek, chopped
3½ oz (100 g) lightly cured smoked salmon, finely sliced into strips
12 oz (350 g), peeled weight, potatoes, cut into ¹⁄₁₆-inch (2-mm) slices
2 tbsp finely chopped fresh chives
2 tbsp finely chopped fresh dill
1 tbsp finely chopped fresh tarragon
2 tsp whole grain mustard
pepper, to taste
1¼ oz (35 g) watercress

1. Preheat the oven to 400°F/200°C. Line the bottom of a 7½-inch (19-cm) sandwich pan with waxed paper.
2. Pour the milk into a large, heavy-bottom pan, add the cloves, bay leaves, onion, leek, and smoked salmon and heat over a low heat.
3. When the milk is just about to reach simmering point, carefully remove the smoked salmon with a slotted spoon and let cool on a plate.
4. Add the potatoes to the milk and stir with a wooden spoon. Return to a simmer and cook, stirring occasionally to prevent the potatoes from sticking, for 12 minutes, or until the potatoes are just beginning to soften and the milk has thickened slightly from the potato starch. Remove the cloves and bay leaves.
5. Add the herbs, mustard, and pepper and stir well. Pour the mixture into the prepared pan. Cover with a layer of waxed paper and then foil and bake in the oven for 30 minutes.
6. Remove from the oven and place a pan on top. Let cool for 20 minutes before turning out onto a baking sheet. Put under a preheated hot broiler to brown the top. Cut the gratin into 6 wedges and serve with the smoked salmon, tossed with the watercress.

COOK'S TIP
• *This gratin can be made in advance and then quickly reheated in the microwave to serve.*

NUTRITION INFORMATION
per serving

calories	fat	sat fat
107	2 g	0.8 g

Tagliatelle with roasted artichokes and horseradish-herb sauce

V | **prep** 15 minutes | **cook** 35 minutes | **serves** 2

3½ oz (100 g), drained weight, canned
   artichokes, quartered
vegetable oil spray
1¾ oz (50 g) fresh baby spinach leaves
3½ oz (100 g) dried tagliatelle
generous ⅓ cup White Sauce (see
   below)
2 tsp chopped fresh basil, plus extra
   to garnish
1 tsp finely chopped fresh lemon
   thyme, plus extra to garnish
1 tsp creamed horseradish
2 tsp 15% fat sour cream

1. Preheat the oven to 425°F/220°C.
2. Spread the artichokes out on a nonstick
baking sheet, spray lightly with oil and
roast in the oven for 20 minutes until
golden brown.
3. Meanwhile, heat a large pan over
medium heat. Add the spinach, cover, and
let steam for 2 minutes. Remove from the
heat and drain the spinach in a colander.
4. Cook the pasta according to the
instructions on the package and drain.
5. Return the drained spinach to the pan,
add the sauce, and warm gently. Add
the herbs, horseradish, sour cream, and
artichokes and stir in the warm pasta.
Allow to warm through.
6. Serve, garnished with extra herbs.

White sauce

V | **prep** 5 minutes | **cook** 10 minutes | **serves** 2

generous 1 cup skim milk
⅛ cup cornstarch
1 tsp mustard powder
2 small bay leaves
1 small onion
4 tsp freshly grated vegetarian
   Parmesan or romano cheese
4¼ oz (120 g) baby spinach leaves

1. To make the sauce, put the milk into a
small, nonstick pan with the flour, mustard,
onion, and bay leaf. Whisk over medium heat
until thick.
2. Remove from the heat, discard the onion,
and bay leaf and stir in the cheese. Set aside,
stirring occasionally, to prevent a skin forming.

NUTRITION INFORMATION
per serving

calories	fat	sat fat
245	4.5 g	0.6 g

Pasta with spiced leek, butternut squash, and cherry tomatoes

(V) | **prep** 15 minutes | **cook** 25 minutes | serves 4

5½ oz (150 g) baby leeks, cut into ¾-inch (2-cm) slices
6 oz (175 g), peeled weight, butternut squash, seeded and cut into
   ¾-inch (2-cm) chunks
1½ tbsp medium ready-prepared curry paste
1 tsp canola or vegetable oil
6 oz (175 g) cherry tomatoes
9 oz (250 g) dried pasta of your choice
1¼ cups White Sauce (see page 45)
2 tbsp chopped fresh cilantro leaves

1. Preheat the oven to 400°F/200°C.
2. Bring a large pan of water to a boil, add the leeks, and cook for 2 minutes. Add the butternut squash and cook for an additional 2 minutes. Drain in a colander.
3. Mix the curry paste with the oil in a large bowl. Toss the leeks and butternut squash in the mixture to coat thoroughly.
4. Transfer the leeks and butternut squash to a nonstick baking sheet and roast in the oven for 10 minutes until golden brown. Add the tomatoes and roast for an additional 5 minutes.
5. Meanwhile, cook the pasta according to the instructions on the package and drain.
6. Put the sauce into a large pan and warm over low heat. Add the leeks, butternut squash, tomatoes, and cilantro and stir in the warm pasta. Mix thoroughly and serve.

NUTRITION INFORMATION

per serving

calories	fat	sat fat
291	3 g	0.5 g

Thai chicken salad

prep 30 minutes + 2 hours standing │ **cook** 15 minutes │ **serves** 6

vegetable oil spray
4 oz (115 g) skinless chicken breast, cut lengthwise horizontally
3 limes, halved, for squeezing over

for the dressing
1 tbsp finely shredded lemongrass
1 small green chili, finely chopped
3 tbsp lime juice
½-inch (1-cm) galangal or gingerroot, peeled and thinly sliced into strips
1½ tsp sugar
2 tbsp white wine vinegar
⅓ cup water
1½ tsp cornstarch, blended with a little cold water

for the salad
1¾ oz (50 g) seeded mixed bell peppers, finely sliced into strips
1¾ oz (50 g), peeled weight, carrot, finely sliced into strips
1¾ oz (50 g) zucchini, finely sliced into strips
1¾ oz (50 g) snow peas, finely sliced into strips
1¾ oz (50 g) baby corn, finely sliced into strips
1¾ oz (50 g) broccoli florets, cut into ¼-inch (5-mm) pieces
1¾ oz (50 g) bok choy, shredded
4 tbsp coarsely chopped fresh cilantro leaves
1 oz (25 g) rice vermicelli, covered with boiling water, left to cool in the water, and drained

1. To make the dressing, put all the dressing ingredients, except the cornstarch, into a small pan over low heat and bring to the boil. Gradually add the cornstarch mixture, stirring constantly, and cook until thickened. Remove from the heat and let cool.
2. Heat a stovetop grill pan over high heat and spray lightly with oil. Add the chicken and cook for 2 minutes on each side, or until thoroughly cooked through. Remove the chicken from the pan and shred.
3. To make the salad, put all the salad ingredients with the chicken into a large bowl. Pour over the dressing and toss together, making sure that all the ingredients are well coated.
4. Cover and refrigerate for at least 2 hours before serving. Serve on large plates, squeezing the juice from half a lime over each portion.

NUTRITION INFORMATION

per serving

calories	fat	sat fat
134	1.5 g	0.4 g

Stuffed eggplants with ruby chard and spinach salad

(V) | **prep** 40 minutes + 8 hours soaking | **cook** 2 hours | **serves** 4

6 oz (175 g) canned cranberry beans
9 oz (250 g) cherry tomatoes, halved
8 baby eggplants, or 2 eggplants, halved
vegetable oil spray
½ tsp cumin seeds
½ tsp coriander seeds
2 tsp ground cinnamon
¼ tsp dried marjoram
2 tsp crushed garlic
½ tsp finely chopped red chili
½ tsp vegetable oil
2 oz (50 g), peeled weight, onion, finely chopped

3 tbsp chopped fresh dill
3 tbsp chopped fresh mint
juice of 1 lemon
pepper, to taste

for the salad
1 tbsp white wine vinegar
pepper, to taste
pinch of cayenne pepper
1 tbsp extra virgin olive oil
2¼ oz (60 g) mixed ruby chard and fresh spinach leaves

1. Drain the beans and rinse under cold water for 2 minutes to remove the salt.
2. Preheat the oven to 375°F/190°C.
3. Arrange the tomatoes and eggplants in a roasting pan, spray lightly with vegetable oil and roast in the oven for 7–8 minutes. Remove the tomatoes and let cool on a plate. Roast the eggplants for an additional 10–12 minutes, or until tender.
4. Meanwhile, pound the cumin and coriander seeds, cinnamon, marjoram, garlic, and chili to a smooth paste in a mortar with a pestle.
5. Remove the eggplants from the oven, let cool slightly, then cut in half lengthwise and scoop the flesh into a bowl using a teaspoon, reserving the skins.
6. Heat a nonstick skillet over medium heat, add the vegetable oil, and cook the onion until golden brown. Add the spice paste and cook for 2 minutes. Add the eggplant pulp, beans, herbs, lemon juice, and pepper and mash together using a fork. Remove from the heat and let cool.
7. Put 3½ oz (100 g) of the cherry tomatoes into a bowl with the vinegar, pepper, cayenne, and olive oil and blend with a hand-held electric blender, or use a food processor. Pass the dressing through a fine strainer.
8. Fill the eggplant skins with the bean mixture, then place 2 tomato halves on each filled skin and transfer to a nonstick baking sheet. Heat in the oven for 10 minutes.
9. Arrange the ruby chard and spinach on a serving plate, drizzle with the tomato dressing, and top with the eggplants.

NUTRITION INFORMATION
per serving

calories	fat	sat fat
111	5 g	0.7 g

Roasted bell pepper and garlic dressing

V | prep 15 minutes | cook 30 minutes | serves 8

3 oz (85 g) seeded red bell pepper, halved
½ tsp canola or vegetable oil
2 tbsp sliced garlic
1 tbsp coriander seeds
1 tsp cumin seeds
2 tsp chopped fresh rosemary
generous ⅓ cup water
1 tsp sugar
¼ tsp smoked paprika
1 tbsp white wine vinegar
1 tbsp cornstarch, blended with a little cold water

1. Preheat the oven to 400°F/200°C. Put the bell pepper on a nonstick baking sheet and roast in the oven until the skin blisters. Remove from the oven, let cool, then peel off the skin.
2. Heat the oil in a small pan over medium heat, add the garlic and cook, stirring constantly, until golden brown. Add the coriander and cumin and cook for 1 minute, stirring. Add the rosemary, water, sugar, paprika, and vinegar and bring to a boil. Gradually add the cornstarch, stirring constantly, and cook until thickened.
3. Add the roasted bell pepper. Using a hand-held electric blender, blend until smooth, or use a food processor.
4. Pass through a fine strainer, cover with plastic wrap to prevent a skin forming, and let cool.
5. Keep the dressing in the refrigerator. Serve tossed with mixed salad greens to accompany broiled chicken and fish dishes.

NUTRITION INFORMATION

per serving

calories	fat	sat fat
15	0.6 g	0.0 g

Pink grapefruit, raspberry, wasabi, and pumpkin seed oil dressing

V | prep 15 minutes | cook 5 minutes | serves 12

1 pink grapefruit
generous ¼ cup water
1 tbsp white wine vinegar
1 tsp sugar
1 tbsp cornstarch, blended with a little cold water
25 g raspberries
¼ tsp wasabi paste
1 tsp toasted sesame seed oil

1. Working over a bowl to catch the juice, halve the grapefruit, then cut out the segments between the membranes. Weigh out and set aside 3 oz (85 g) segments. Squeeze and measure out ⅓ cup juice from the remaining grapefruit segments.
2. Put the grapefruit juice, water, vinegar, and sugar into a small pan over medium heat and bring to a boil.
3. Gradually add the cornstarch mixture, stirring constantly, and cook until thickened. Remove from the heat and add the reserved grapefruit segments, raspberries, wasabi paste, and oil.
4. Using a hand-held electric blender, blend the mixture until smooth, or use a food processor. Pass through a fine strainer. Cover with plastic wrap to prevent a skin forming and let chill in the refrigerator. Keep the dressing in the refrigerator until ready to use.
5. Use with shredded vegetables or fruits to make a delicious salad, or as a sauce to accompany salmon dishes.

NUTRITION INFORMATION

per serving

calories	fat	sat fat
13	0.3 g	0.0 g

53

Spiced lamb and butternut burger with saffron and cucumber raita

prep 30 minutes + 1 hour cooling/chilling | cook 30–35 minutes | serves 2

for the burgers
1¾ oz (50 g), peeled weight, butternut squash, seeded and cut into
 ¼-inch (5-mm) cubes
2 small crushed garlic cloves
1½ oz (40 g), peeled weight, onion, finely chopped
1 tbsp chopped fresh basil
pinch of ground cumin
pinch of crushed coriander seeds
pinch of chili powder
½ tsp dried marjoram
½ egg white
2¾ oz (75 g) leg of lamb, all visible fat removed, ground or finely chopped

for the raita
1¾ oz (50 g) cucumber
4 tbsp 0% fat strained plain yogurt
pinch of saffron threads, soaked in a little warm water for 15 minutes

for the garnish
1 beefsteak tomato, halved
1 small whole wheat bread roll, halved
½ oz (15 g) mixed salad greens
½ lemon, for squeezing over the burgers

1. Preheat the oven to 350°F/180°C.
2. Spread the butternut squash out on a nonstick baking sheet and cook in the oven for 15–20 minutes, or until tender. Remove and let cool on a plate.
3. Meanwhile, to make the raita, grate the cucumber into a small bowl, add the yogurt and saffron and mix together. Cover and let chill in the refrigerator.
4. Dry-sweat the garlic and onion in a skillet for 3-4 minutes, or until soft.
5. Using a fork, mash the cold butternut squash in a bowl, then add the basil, cumin, coriander, chili powder, marjoram, egg white, and lamb together with the garlic and onion. Mix thoroughly, form into 2 equal-size burgers and put on a nonstick baking sheet.
6. Preheat the broiler. Broil the burgers and tomato for 4–5 minutes on each side, or until the burgers are cooked through and the tomato is golden brown.
7. Lightly toast the bread roll halves.
8. Serve each burger on a bread roll half with the broiled tomato and salad greens. Squeeze over a little lemon. Serve the raita separately.

NUTRITION INFORMATION

per serving

calories	fat	sat fat
165	4.5 g	2 g

Most of us still consider that meat and fish should constitute the main part of a meal, but in fact we all tend to eat far too much protein and the body needs a lot less than we imagine. Consider the food on your plate as a whole picture,

Meat and fish main

with meat or fish forming just one part of a healthy, nutritious meal. If you divide your plate into three equal segments of protein, carbohydrates, and vegetables, you will achieve a more balanced approach to eating. It is also important that the flavors of all three components complement each other and that they are achieved as naturally as possible.

Always choose the freshest, best-quality meat and fish you can buy to enjoy their natural flavors to the full. We have become overreliant on one seasoning in particular: salt, which is not only overused in processed food but during cooking and at the table. Use healthy alternatives such as citrus juices, vinegars, spices, and herbs. You will be surprised how quickly your body stops craving salt and within a couple of weeks you will find yourself no longer needing to reach for the saltshaker.

courses

Chicken kabobs with Asian coleslaw, fragrant rice, and spicy dipping sauce

prep 30 minutes + 1 hour marinating/soaking/cooling | **cook** 10 minutes | **serves** 2

6 oz (175 g) chicken fillets
½ cup fragrant Thai rice
vegetable oil spray

for the chicken marinade
1 tbsp finely chopped lemongrass
1 tsp grated gingerroot
½ tsp grated garlic
¼ tsp ground turmeric
½ tsp finely chopped red chili
1 tbsp lime juice
½ tsp sugar

for the dipping sauce
generous ⅓ cup unsweetened
   pineapple juice
1 tbsp white wine vinegar
¼ tsp grated gingerroot

½ tsp finely chopped red chili
1 tbsp finely chopped scallion
½ tsp arrowroot, blended with a little
   cold water
¼ tsp toasted sesame oil
1 tbsp chopped fresh cilantro leaves

for the coleslaw
1¾ oz (50 g) bok choy, shredded
1½ oz (40 g), peeled weight, carrot,
   finely sliced into strips
2¼ oz (60 g), peeled weight, daikon,
   finely sliced into strips
1½ oz (40 g) seeded red bell pepper,
   finely sliced into strips

1. To make the marinade, mix all the ingredients together in a large bowl. Add the chicken fillets and toss well to coat. Cover and let marinate in the refrigerator for 30 minutes, turning occasionally.
2. Meanwhile, to make the dipping sauce, put all the ingredients, except the arrowroot mixture, sesame oil, and cilantro, into a small pan over medium heat and bring to a boil. Using a hand whisk, gradually beat the arrowroot mixture into the boiling liquid, whisking constantly until thickened. Remove the pan from the heat and stir in the sesame oil and cilantro. Let cool.
3. Soak 6 bamboo skewers in cold water for 30 minutes, then thread the chicken fillets, concertina-style, onto the skewers. Cover and refrigerate until ready to cook.
4. Cook the rice according to the instructions on the package and drain.
5. Meanwhile, to make the coleslaw, mix all the ingredients together in a large bowl with half the dipping sauce, then spoon onto a serving dish.
6. Preheat the broiler to hot. Transfer the chicken skewers to a nonstick baking sheet and broil for 4 minutes on each side, or until cooked through. Serve on top of the coleslaw, with the rice and dipping sauce served separately.

NUTRITION INFORMATION

per serving

calories	fat	sat fat
348	6 g	1.5 g

Duck breast with noodles and crunchy rice topping

prep 35 minutes + 10 minutes soaking | cook 1¹/₄ hours | serves 4

generous ¼ cup freshly squeezed orange juice
generous ⅓ cup water
2 tsp crushed garlic
1 tsp finely chopped gingerroot
2 star anise
¼ tsp Szechuan pepper
2 tsp grated orange zest
1 tsp sugar
2 duck breasts, skin and any visible fat removed
⅛ cup, dry weight, white rice
½ tsp cornstarch, blended with a little cold water
½ tsp sesame oil
3½ oz (100 g) Napa cabbage, shredded
generous 1 cup bean sprouts
5½ oz (150 g) seeded mixed bell peppers, finely sliced into strips
1 oz (25 g) scallion, finely sliced into strips
8¾ oz (240 g), dry weight, egg noodles, refreshed in cold water and drained

for the garnish
4 tbsp scallion, shredded
4 tbsp chopped fresh cilantro leaves

1. Preheat the oven to 400°F/200°C.
2. Put the orange juice, water, garlic, ginger, spices, orange zest, and sugar into a small pan and bring to a boil. Reduce the heat and simmer for 3–4 minutes.
3. Lay the duck in a small, ovenproof dish and pour over the orange mixture. Cover with a tight-fitting lid or foil and cook in the oven for 1 hour.
4. Soak the rice in cold water for 10 minutes, drain, and pat dry with paper towels. Heat a small, nonstick skillet over medium heat, add the rice, and dry-fry until golden brown. Remove from the heat, tip onto one half of a clean dish towel, then fold the other half over the rice. Using a rolling pin, crush into fine grains.
5. Remove the duck from the cooking liquid with a slotted spoon, shred, and keep warm. Transfer the cooking liquid to a pan over medium heat. Gradually add the cornstarch mixture, stirring constantly, and cook until thickened. Pass through a strainer into a bowl and keep warm.
6. Heat a wok over high heat, then add the oil. Add the vegetables and stir-fry for a few minutes until cooked. Add the noodles, duck, and sauce and briefly stir-fry. Serve in warmed bowls, garnished with scallion and cilantro and sprinkled with the rice.

NUTRITION INFORMATION

per serving

calories	fat	sat fat
250	6.5 g	2 g

Braised lamb with pea salsa and quinoa tabbouleh

prep 30 minutes | cook 1 hour | serves 4

4 x 2¼ oz (60 g) leg of lamb steaks, all
 visible fat removed
1¾ oz (50 g), peeled weight, onion,
 finely chopped
1 garlic clove, peeled and finely chopped
2 bay leaves
2 sprigs of rosemary
generous ⅓ cup water
2 tbsp red wine
generous 1 cup strained canned
 tomatoes

for the pea salsa
1½ oz (40 g) green beans, cut into
 ¼-inch (5-mm) pieces
1½ oz (40 g) shelled peas

1½ oz (40 g) sugar snap peas, cut into
 ¼-inch (5-mm) pieces
1½ oz (40 g) snow peas, cut into
 ¼-inch (5-mm) pieces
2 tbsp balsamic vinegar
½ tsp Dijon mustard

for the quinoa tabbouleh
2½ cups water
generous ⅓ cup, dry weight, quinoa
scant ⅓ cup, dry weight, bulgur wheat
1 tsp ready-made mint sauce
 from a jar
1 tbsp lemon juice
1¾ oz (50 g) tomato, peeled, seeded
 and cut into ¼-inch (5-mm) pieces

1. Preheat the oven to 350°F/180°C.
2. Using a rolling pin or mallet, gently beat the lamb steaks between 2 layers of plastic wrap to ⅟₁₆ inch (2 mm) thick, then roll up to form olives, folding in the ends to neaten.
3. Heat an ovenproof casserole dish over medium heat, add the onion, garlic, bay leaves, and rosemary and cook until the onion is softened. Add the water, wine, and strained canned tomatoes, then lay the olives on top and bring to a boil. Cover and cook in the oven for 45 minutes, or until the meat is tender.
4. Meanwhile, to make the salsa, blanch the vegetables, refresh in cold water until cold, and drain. Mix the vinegar and mustard together in a microwaveproof container, add the vegetables, and toss to coat.
5. To make the tabbouleh, bring the water to a boil in a pan, add the quinoa and bulgur wheat and cook for 12 minutes. Drain, tip into a separate microwaveproof container with the mint sauce, lemon juice, and tomato, and mix well.
6. Remove the olives from the casserole with a slotted spoon and keep warm. Reduce the sauce over heat until thick and syrupy.
7. Reheat the tabbouleh and salsa in a microwave oven on full power for 1½ minutes. Put the olives on top of the tabbouleh, pour over the sauce, and serve with salsa.

NUTRITION INFORMATION

per serving

calories	fat	sat fat
200	4 g	1.5 g

Lean 'n' mean Jamaican jerk pork chops with rice, black-eye peas, and roasted squash

prep 20 minutes | **cook** 30 minutes | **serves** 4

3 oz (85 g), peeled weight, onion, finely chopped
3 oz (85 g) seeded red bell pepper, cut into ¼-inch (5-mm) squares
2 bay leaves
2 mace blades
scant ⅓ cup easy-cook long-grain rice
1½ cups chicken stock
½ cup cooked black-eye peas
pepper, to taste
9½ oz (275 g) squash, seeded but left unpeeled and cut into
    ½-inch (1-cm) wedges
4 x 4 oz (115 g) pork loin chops, all visible fat removed and the bone trimmed
canola or vegetable oil spray
½ lemon, cut into wedges, for squeezing over

for the jerk spice rub
1 tsp sugar
½ tsp dried oregano
½ tsp paprika
½ tsp ground cinnamon
¼ tsp chili powder
½ tsp crushed garlic
¼ tsp ground allspice
1 tbsp lemon juice

1. Preheat the oven to 400°F/200°C.
2. Heat a medium pan over high heat, add the onion and bell pepper and cook
for 2 minutes, stirring constantly. Add the bay leaves and mace, then stir in the rice, stock,
beans, and pepper. Cover, bring to a simmer, and cook for 12–15 minutes, or until the rice
has absorbed the stock and is tender. Remove from the heat and keep warm.
3. Meanwhile, spread the squash out on a nonstick baking sheet and cook in the oven for
15 minutes, turning occasionally, until golden brown.
4. To make the jerk spice rub, mix all the ingredients in a bowl and rub into the pork.
5. Heat a stovetop grill pan over medium heat and spray lightly with oil. Sear the chops on
both sides, then cook for 4–5 minutes on each side, or until thoroughly cooked through. Do
not let the pan become too hot as it will burn the spice mix before the meat is cooked.
6. Serve the chops with the rice and beans and the roasted squash, squeezing the lemon
over the meat.

NUTRITION INFORMATION

per serving

calories	fat	sat fat
300	9 g	3 g

Sweet-and-sour sea bass

prep 25 minutes + 30 minutes cooling | **cook** 15 minutes | **serves** 2

2¼ oz (60 g) bok choy, shredded
generous ¼ cup bean sprouts
1½ oz (40 g) shiitake mushrooms, sliced
1½ oz (40 g) oyster mushrooms, torn
¾ oz (20 g) scallion, finely sliced
1 tsp finely grated gingerroot
1 tbsp finely sliced lemongrass
2 x 3¼ oz (2 x 90 g) sea bass fillets, skinned and boned
1 tbsp sesame seeds, toasted

for the sweet-and-sour sauce
⅓ cup unsweetened pineapple juice
1 tbsp sugar
1 tbsp red wine vinegar
2 star anise, crushed
⅓ cup tomato juice
1 tbsp cornstarch, blended with a little cold water

1. Preheat the oven to 400°F/200°C. Cut 2 x 15-inch (38-cm) squares of waxed paper and 2 of the same size aluminum foil squares.
2. To make the sauce, heat the pineapple juice, sugar, red wine vinegar, star anise, and tomato juice in a pan, let simmer for 1–2 minutes then thicken with the cornstarch and water mixture, whisking constantly, then pass through a fine strainer into a small bowl to cool.
3. In a separate large bowl mix together the bok choy, bean sprouts, mushrooms, and scallions, then add the ginger and lemongrass. Toss all the ingredients together.
4. Put a square of waxed paper on top of a square of foil and fold into a triangle. Open up and place half the vegetable mix into the center, pour half the sweet-and-sour sauce over the vegetables and place the sea bass on top. Sprinkle with a few sesame seeds. Close the triangle over the mixture and, starting at the top, fold the right corner and crumple the edges together to form an airtight triangular bag. Repeat to make the second bag.
5. Place onto a baking sheet and cook in the oven for 10 minutes until the foil bags puff with steam. To serve, place on individual plates and snip open at the table so that you can enjoy the wonderful aromas as the bag is opened.

NUTRITION INFORMATION
per serving

calories	fat	sat fat
150	3 g	0.5 g

Blackened snapper with corn papaya relish

prep 20 minutes + 45 minutes cooling | **cook** 20 minutes | **serves** 4

4 x 3 oz (85 g) snapper fillets
vegetable oil spray
2 lemons, halved, to serve

for the relish
2 tbsp finely chopped onion
1 tsp sugar
2 tbsp white wine vinegar
2 tbsp cooked or canned corn kernels
¼ tsp finely chopped habanero chili or other type of chili
generous ⅓ cup water
¼ tsp yellow mustard seeds
pinch of ground turmeric
1 tsp cornstarch, blended with a little cold water
1¾ oz (50 g) papaya, cut into ¼-inch (5-mm) cubes

for the seasoning mix
¼ tsp paprika
½ tsp onion powder
¼ tsp dried thyme
¼ tsp dried oregano
¼ tsp cayenne pepper
¼ tsp ground black pepper
½ tsp cornstarch

1. To make the relish, place the onion, sugar, vinegar, corn, chili, water, mustard seeds, and turmeric into a small pan over medium heat and bring to a boil. Let simmer for 10 minutes, then add the cornstarch mixture, stirring constantly, and cook until it is the required consistency (it will thicken slightly when cooled). Stir in the papaya and let cool.
2. To make the seasoning mix, put all the ingredients into a small bowl and mix thoroughly.
3. Sprinkle the seasoning mix over the snapper fillets on both sides and pat into the flesh, then shake off any excess. Lay the fillets on a cutting board.
4. Heat a nonstick skillet over high heat until smoking. Lightly spray both sides of the fillets with oil, then put into the hot pan and cook for 2 minutes. Turn the fillets and cook all the way through. (If the fillets are thick, finish the cooking under a preheated broiler as the less intense heat will prevent the seasoning mix from burning.) Remove the fish from the skillet.
5. Add the lemon halves, cut-side down, and cook over high heat for 2–5 minutes until browned. Serve the fillets, topped with relish, on warmed plates, with the lemon halves.

NUTRITION INFORMATION

per serving

calories	fat	sat fat
100	2 g	0.3 g

Salmon and shrimp egg rolls with plum sauce

prep 30 minutes + 45 minutes cooling | **cook** 25 minutes | **serves** 4

4½ oz (125 g) salmon fillet, skinned, boned and cut into ⅛-inch (3-mm) cubes
generous ⅜ cup bean sprouts
2¼ oz (60 g) Napa cabbage, finely shredded
1 oz (25 g) scallion, finely chopped
2¼ oz (60 g) seeded red bell pepper, finely sliced into strips
¼ tsp five-spice powder
2¼ oz (60 g) cooked shrimps, shelled
4 egg roll skins, halved widthwise
vegetable oil spray
¼ tsp sesame seeds

for the plum sauce
generous ⅓ cup water
¼ cup freshly squeezed orange juice
½ tsp chopped red chili
1 tsp peeled and grated gingerroot
7 oz (200 g), pitted weight, red plums
1 tsp chopped scallion
1 tsp chopped fresh cilantro leaves
¼ tsp sesame oil

1. Preheat the oven to 350°F/180°C.
2. To make the sauce, put the water, orange juice, chili, ginger, and plums into a medium-size pan and bring to a boil. Reduce the heat, cover, and let simmer for 10 minutes. Remove from the heat, blend with a hand-held electric blender, or use a food processor, then stir in the scallion, cilantro, and sesame oil. Let cool.
3. Heat a nonstick wok over high heat, add the salmon, and stir-fry for 1 minute. Remove from the wok with a slotted spoon onto a plate. Using the cooking juices from the salmon, stir-fry the vegetables with the five-spice powder until just tender, drain in a colander, then stir in the cooked salmon and shrimps—the mixture should be quite dry to prevent the dough from becoming soggy.
4. Divide the salmon and vegetable mixture into 8 portions. Spoon each portion along one short edge of each dough rectangle and roll up, tucking in the sides.
5. Lay the egg rolls on a nonstick baking sheet and spray lightly with vegetable oil, sprinkle with sesame seeds, and bake in the oven for 12–15 minutes, or until golden brown.
6. Serve the egg rolls with the cold plum sauce separately.

NUTRITION INFORMATION

per serving

calories	fat	sat fat
140	5 g	1 g

Vegetarian food can be both flavorsome and healthy, but in many respects a little more thought and planning is required in its preparation, since it often relies too heavily on high-fat foods such as dairy products and nuts, which although very nutritious contain high levels of fat.

Vegetarian main

The same nutritional principles apply to a vegetarian diet as to a nonvegetarian diet—eat a wide variety of foods including lots of cereals, vegetables, fruit, and moderate amounts of protein. And don't forget that vegetarian food is not only for vegetarians—carnivores can also enjoy its considerable culinary delights.

courses

Spiced risotto cakes with mango, lime, and cream cheese

(V) | prep 30 minutes + 30 minutes cooling | cook 45–50 minutes | serves 3

3 oz (85 g), peeled weight, onion, finely chopped
3 oz (85 g) leek, finely chopped
⅛ cup risotto rice
scant 2½ cups vegetable stock
scant ½ cup grated zucchini
1 tbsp fresh basil, chopped
½ cup fresh whole wheat breadcrumbs
vegetable oil spray

for the filling
scant ¼ cup 4% fat cream cheese
1¾ oz (50 g), peeled weight, mango, diced
1 tsp finely grated lime zest
1 tsp lime juice
pinch of cayenne pepper

1. Preheat the oven to 400°F/200°C.
2. Heat a large, nonstick pan over high heat, add the onion and leek, and cook, stirring constantly, for 2–3 minutes, or until softened but not colored.
3. Add the rice and stock, bring to the boil, then continue to boil, stirring constantly, for 2 minutes. Reduce the heat and cook for an additional 15 minutes, stirring every 2–3 minutes.
4. When the rice is nearly cooked and has absorbed all the stock, stir in the zucchini and basil and cook, continuing to stir, over high heat for an additional 5–10 minutes or until the mixture is sticky and dry. Turn out onto a plate and let cool.
5. Meanwhile, to make the filling, mix the cream cheese, mango, lime zest and juice, and cayenne together in a bowl.
6. Divide the cooled rice mixture into 3 and form into cakes. Make an indentation in the center of each cake and fill with 1 tbsp of the filling. Mold the sides up and over to seal in the filling, then reshape with a palette knife. Coat each cake with bread crumbs and arrange on a nonstick baking sheet.
7. Spray each cake lightly with oil and bake in the oven for 15–20 minutes, or until a light golden brown color. Serve with salad greens.

COOK'S TIP
• *It is important to use a really starchy rice like risotto rice so that the cakes hold together during reheating. Stirring the rice breaks down the starch and helps with the molding.*

NUTRITION INFORMATION

per serving

calories	fat	sat fat
113	2.5 g	0.8 g

Lentil bolognaise

(V) | **prep** 25 minutes | **cook** 20–25 minutes | **serves** 4

1 tsp canola or vegetable oil
1 tsp crushed garlic
1 oz (25 g), peeled weight, onion, finely chopped
1 oz (25 g) leek, finely chopped
1 oz (25 g) celery, finely chopped
1 oz (25 g) seeded green bell pepper, finely chopped
1 oz (25 g), peeled weight, carrot, finely chopped
1 oz (25 g) zucchini, finely chopped
3 oz (85 g) flat mushrooms, diced
4 tbsp red wine
pinch of dried thyme
14 oz (400 g) canned tomatoes, chopped, strained through a colander, and the
    juice and pulp reserved separately
4 tbsp dried Puy (French green) lentils, cooked (see COOK'S TIP)
pepper, to taste
2 tsp lemon juice
1 tsp sugar
3 tbsp chopped fresh basil, plus extra sprigs to garnish
5 oz (140 g) dried spaghetti

1. Heat a pan over low heat, add the oil and garlic, and cook, stirring, until golden brown. Add all the vegetables, except the mushrooms, increase the heat to medium, and cook, stirring occasionally, for 10–12 minutes, or until softened and there is no liquid from the vegetables left in the pan. Add the mushrooms.
2. Increase the heat to high, add the wine, and cook for 2 minutes. Add the thyme and juice from the tomatoes and cook until reduced by half.
3. Add the lentils and pepper, stir in the tomatoes, and cook for an additional 3–4 minutes.
4. Meanwhile, cook the spaghetti according to the instructions on the package.
5. Remove the pan from the heat and stir in the lemon juice, sugar, and basil.
6. Serve the sauce with the cooked spaghetti, garnished with basil sprigs.

COOK'S TIP

• *Puy or French green lentils can be cooked without presoaking. Rinse thoroughly, cover in fresh cold water, and cook for 25–30 minutes, or until just tender.*

NUTRITION INFORMATION
per serving

calories	fat	sat fat
210	2 g	0.2 g

Thai yellow vegetable curry with brown basmati rice

(V) | **prep** 35 minutes | **cook** 25 minutes | **serves** 4

1¾ oz (50 g) seeded yellow bell pepper, cut into ½-inch (1-cm) squares
1¾ oz (50 g) celery, cut into ¼-inch (5-mm) lengths
1¾ oz (50 g) baby corn, cut into ¼-inch (5-mm) lengths
3 oz (85 g) leek, cut into ¼-inch (5-mm) lengths
3½ oz (100 g), peeled weight, sweet potato, cut into ½-inch (1-cm) cubes
1¼ cups pineapple juice
scant 1 cup water
100g (3½ oz) bok choy, shredded
1¾ oz (50 g) zucchini, cut into ¼-inch (5-mm) cubes
1¾ oz (50 g) snow peas, thinly sliced into strips
3 tbsp lime juice
2 tbsp cornstarch, blended with a little cold water
4 tbsp lowfat plain yogurt
4 tbsp chopped fresh cilantro leaves
generous ¾ cup cooked brown basmati rice

for the spice mix
1 tsp finely chopped garlic
¼ tsp ground turmeric
1 tsp ground coriander
1 tsp finely chopped lemongrass
3 kaffir lime leaves
1 tsp finely chopped green chili

1. To make the spice mix, pound all the spices to a fine paste using a pestle in a mortar.
2. Put the bell pepper, celery, baby corn, leek, sweet potato, pineapple juice, water, and the spice mix into a large saucepan and bring to a boil. Reduce the heat and skim the scum from the surface with a metal spoon. Cover and let simmer for 15 minutes.
3. Add the bok choy, zucchini, and snow peas and cook for 2 minutes.
4. Add the lime juice, then gradually add the cornstarch mixture, stirring constantly, and cook until thickened to the required consistency.
5. Remove the curry from the heat and let cool for 2–3 minutes. Stir in the yogurt. (Do not boil once the yogurt has been added or the curry will separate.)
6. Stir in the fresh cilantro and serve the curry with the rice, garnished with a little extra fresh cilantro.

NUTRITION INFORMATION

per serving

calories	fat	sat fat
235	1 g	0.2 g

Tofu moussaka

(V) | **prep** 30 minutes | **cook** 1 hour 30–35 minutes | **serves** 4

2 x 2¾ oz (2 x 75 g) baking potatoes, scrubbed
4 tbsp lemon juice
1 tsp canola or vegetable oil
1 tsp sugar
2 tsp crushed garlic
1 tsp ground cumin
2 tbsp dried oregano
9 oz (250 g) eggplant, diced
3½ oz (100 g), peeled weight, onion, sliced
6 oz (175 g) seeded mixed bell peppers, diced
7 oz (200 g) canned tomatoes, chopped
1¼ cups 0% fat plain yogurt
2 tbsp cornstarch
2 tbsp English mustard powder
7 oz (200 g) silken tofu, sliced
3 oz (85 g) beefsteak tomato, cut into ⅛-inch (3-mm) slices

1. Preheat the oven to 375°F/190°C.
2. Bake the potatoes in their skins in the oven for 45 minutes, then remove and cut into ⅛-inch (3-mm) slices.
3. Mix the lemon juice, oil, sugar, garlic, cumin, and oregano together in a small bowl, then lightly brush over the diced eggplant, reserving the remaining mixture. Spread out on a nonstick baking sheet and bake in the oven for 15 minutes.
4. Heat the reserved lemon juice mixture in a small pan over high heat, add the onion and bell peppers, and cook, stirring occasionally, until lightly browned. Add the canned tomatoes, reduce the heat, and simmer for 4 minutes.
5. In a separate pan, whisk the yogurt and cornstarch together, then bring to a boil, whisking constantly until the yogurt boils and thickens (you must whisk constantly or the yogurt will separate before thickening). When the yogurt has thickened, remove from the heat and whisk in the mustard powder.
6. In an ovenproof dish, make as many separate layers of the ingredients as you can, with sauce in between, such as tofu, sauce, onion, and bell peppers, sauce, eggplant, sauce, potato, sauce, and tofu, then finish with a layer of beefsteak tomato topped with sauce.
7. Bake in the oven for 20–25 minutes, or until golden brown on top.

NUTRITION INFORMATION

per serving

calories	fat	sat fat
255	5.5 g	1 g

Rustic roasted ratatouille and potato wedges with smoked paprika and cream cheese

Ⓥ | prep 30 minutes | cook 1 hour | serves 4

10½ oz (300 g) potatoes in their skins, scrubbed
7 oz (200 g) eggplant, cut into ½-inch (1-cm) wedges
4½ oz (125 g), peeled weight, red onion cut into ¼-inch (5-mm) rings
7 oz (200 g) seeded mixed bell peppers, sliced into ½-inch (1-cm) strips
6 oz (175 g) zucchini, cut in half lengthwise, then into ½-inch (1-cm) slices
4½ oz (125 g) cherry tomatoes
scant ½ cup 0% fat cream cheese
1 tsp honey
pinch of smoked paprika
1 tsp chopped fresh parsley

for the marinade
1 tsp canola or vegetable oil
1 tbsp lemon juice
4 tbsp white wine
1 tsp sugar
2 tbsp chopped fresh basil
1 tsp finely chopped fresh rosemary
1 tbsp finely chopped fresh lemon thyme
¼ tsp smoked paprika

1. Preheat the oven to 400°F/200°C.
2. Bake the potatoes in their skins in the oven for 30 minutes, remove, and cut into wedges—the flesh should not be completely cooked.
3. To make the marinade, put all the ingredients into a bowl and blend together with a hand-held electric blender until smooth, or use a food processor.
4. Put the potato wedges into a large bowl with the eggplant, onion, bell peppers, and zucchini, pour over the marinade, and mix thoroughly.
5. Arrange the vegetables on a nonstick baking sheet and roast in the oven, turning occasionally, for 25–30 minutes, or until golden brown and tender. Add the tomatoes for the last 5 minutes of the cooking time just to split the skins and warm slightly.
6. Mix the cream cheese, honey, and paprika together in a bowl.
7. Serve the vegetables with a little of the cream cheese mixture, and sprinkled with chopped parsley.

NUTRITION INFORMATION

per serving

calories	fat	sat fat
200	3 g	1 g

Roasted squash wedges with three-grain risotto, marjoram, and asparagus

(V) | **prep** 20 minutes | **cook** 25 minutes | **serves** 4

1 x 7 oz (200 g) acorn squash or other type of squash, peeled, seeded, and cut into 4 wedges
1 tsp canola or vegetable oil
3½ oz (100 g), peeled weight, onion, finely chopped
1 tsp crushed garlic
2½ oz (70 g) three-grain risotto mix (baldo rice, spelt, and pearl barley—this is available ready-mixed)
2½ cups vegetable stock
8¼ oz (235 g) asparagus tips
2 tbsp finely chopped fresh marjoram, plus extra to garnish
3 tbsp 0% fat cream cheese
2 tbsp finely chopped fresh parsley
pepper, to taste

1. Preheat the oven to 400°F/200°C. Spread out the squash wedges on a nonstick baking sheet and roast in the oven for 20 minutes, or until tender and golden brown.
2. Meanwhile, heat the oil in a medium pan over high heat, add the onion and garlic, and cook, stirring, until softened but not colored. Add the risotto mix and stir in half the stock. Simmer, stirring occasionally, until the stock has reduced in the pan. Pour in the remaining stock and continue to cook, stirring occasionally, until the grains are tender.
3. Cut 6 oz (175 g) of the asparagus into 4-inch (10-cm) lengths and blanch in a pan of boiling water for 2 minutes. Drain and keep warm. Cut the remaining asparagus into ¼-inch (5-mm) slices and add to the risotto for the last 3 minutes of the cooking time.
4. Remove the risotto from the heat and stir in the marjoram, cream cheese, and parsley. Season with pepper. Do not reboil.
5. To serve, lay the squash wedges on warmed serving plates, then spoon over the risotto and top with the asparagus. Garnish with marjoram.

COOK'S TIP

• *The three-grain risotto mix is available from most quality food stores and is ready-prepared, so it needs no presoaking or precooking. If you cannot readily find it, substitute ⅛ cup risotto rice and ⅛ cup pearl barley, precooked for 20 minutes.*

NUTRITION INFORMATION

per serving

calories	fat	sat fat
121	1.5 g	0.2 g

For years we have relied on a pan of boiling salted water to cook our vegetables. This not only has a detrimental effect on the nutritional content of vegetables but it is also the way to turn wonderful fresh

Vegetables and

vegetables into brown unappetizing accompaniments. Roasting, chargrilling, and braising are just three of the different methods of cooking vegetables and will enhance the natural flavors within the vegetables. For instance, next time you cook carrots, don't boil them in water, which only serves to leach all the flavor and the nutrients out of the carrots into the water; instead try roasting them in the oven. This way will remind you of how carrots used to taste.

The general rules are to buy fresh, cook less, and be brave with your combinations, and always remember that the flavorings used within the vegetable or side dish should complement, and not confuse, whatever you serve it with.

side dishes

Kale with sesame, ginger, and scallions

Ⓥ | **prep** 10 minutes | **cook** 15 minutes | **serves** 2

5½ oz (150 g) kale
1 tsp sesame seeds, plus extra
   for sprinkling
1 tsp sugar
1 tbsp peeled and finely sliced
   gingerroot
3 tbsp water
1 tbsp lemon juice
1¾ oz (50 g) scallion, finely sliced
¼ tsp sesame oil

1. Remove all the thick stems from the kale. Bring a large pan of water to a boil. Add the kale, cover, and cook for 6–7 minutes, or until tender. Drain in a colander and keep warm.
2. Heat a small pan over high heat, add the sesame seeds, and cook, tossing the pan, until golden brown.
3. Add the sugar, ginger, water, and lemon juice. Cook until reduced by half, then add the scallion and oil and let simmer for 1 minute.
4. In a large bowl, toss the kale with the sesame seed sauce so that the leaves are well coated.
5. Serve on warmed plates with a few extra sesame seeds sprinkled over the top.

COOK'S TIP
• *This recipe can also be used with other green leaves, broccoli, and green beans. Just blanch and toss in the sesame sauce.*

Roasted beet and shallots with thyme

Ⓥ | **prep** 10 minutes | **cook** 25 minutes | **serves** 4

5½ oz (150 g), peeled weight, shallots,
   left whole
⅛ oz (5 g) sprigs of thyme, plus extra
   to garnish
2 bay leaves
scant 1 cup water
pepper, to taste
9 oz (250 g) cooked beet, peeled and
   cut into 1¼-inch (3-cm) wedges
canola or vegetable oil spray

1. Preheat the oven to 425°F/220°C.
2. Put the shallots, thyme, bay leaves, water, and pepper into a medium-size pan and bring to a boil over high heat. Cook until the liquid is reduced and the sugar in the shallots has made it lightly syrupy.
3. Add the beet and stir to coat in the syrup. Transfer to a nonstick baking sheet.
4. Spray the shallots and beet lightly with the oil and roast in the oven for 20 minutes, turning halfway through, until caramelized.
5. Serve in a warmed serving dish, garnished with thyme sprigs.

COOK'S TIP
• *Try this recipe with fresh rosemary instead of the thyme and serve with your favorite lamb dish.*

NUTRITION INFORMATION
per serving

calories	fat	sat fat
61	3.5 g	0.5 g

NUTRITION INFORMATION
per serving

calories	fat	sat fat
49	1 g	0.1 g

Collard greens, serrano ham, and Jerusalem artichokes

prep 20 minutes | cook 15–20 minutes | serves 4

3½ oz (100 g) Jerusalem artichokes,
  peeled and cut into ¾-inch (2-cm)
  cubes
2 tbsp lemon juice
7 oz (200 g) collard greens, shredded
1 oz (25 g) serrano ham, thinly sliced
  into strips
1 tsp thinly sliced garlic
zest of 1 small lemon, cut into long,
  thin strips with a potato peeler
1 tsp sugar
pepper, to taste

1. Put the Jerusalem artichokes into a
small pan, just cover with water, and add
1 tbsp of the lemon juice. Bring to a boil and
cook for 3 minutes. Drain.
2. Bring a large pan of water to a boil,
add the collard greens, and cook for 3–4
minutes, or until just tender—do not
overcook. Drain.
3. Heat a separate pan over high heat,
add the ham, garlic, and lemon zest, and
stir-fry until golden brown. Stir in the sugar
and remaining lemon juice, then add the
artichokes and cook for 2–3 minutes.
Season with pepper. Remove from the heat
and keep warm.
4. Toss the artichoke mixture with the
collard greens and serve on a warmed
serving plate.

COOK'S TIP
• Use presliced serrano ham in packages
and remove all visible fat from the ham
before cooking.

NUTRITION INFORMATION

per serving

calories	fat	sat fat
58	1 g	0.3 g

Chargrilled fennel with orange and tarragon

(V) prep 15 minutes | cook 30 minutes | serves 4

4 cups water
1 lb 5 oz (600 g) fennel, quartered
4 bay leaves
1 tsp grated orange zest
generous ⅓ cup orange juice
1 tsp fennel seeds
1 tbsp chopped fresh tarragon
1 tsp cornstarch, blended with
  a little cold water
canola or vegetable oil spray
1 x 4½ oz (125 g) orange, peeled and
  quartered

1. Bring the water to a boil in a large
pan and add the fennel and bay leaves.
Reduce the heat, cover, and let simmer for
20 minutes, or until the fennel is tender.
Drain in a colander, discarding the bay
leaves, and keep warm.
2. Meanwhile, put the orange zest and
juice, fennel seeds, and tarragon into a
small pan over high heat and bring to
a boil. Gradually add the cornstarch
mixture, stirring constantly, and cook until
thickened. Remove from the heat, cover
with plastic wrap to prevent a skin forming,
and keep warm.
3. Heat a stovetop grill pan over high heat
and spray lightly with oil. Add the fennel
and cook, turning frequently, until golden
brown on all sides.
4. Add the orange quarters and brown on
both sides.
5. Serve the fennel and orange quarters
with the sauce spooned over.

NUTRITION INFORMATION

per serving

calories	fat	sat fat
40	0.5 g	0.3 g

Roasted carrots with coriander, cumin, and chili

Ⓥ | prep 15 minutes | cook 20–25 minutes | serves 4

10½ oz (300 g) carrots
1 tbsp coriander seeds
1 tsp cumin seeds
1 tsp finely chopped red chili
1 tbsp lemon juice, plus extra to serve
1 tsp canola or vegetable oil
2 tbsp chopped fresh cilantro leaves,
   to garnish

1. Preheat the oven to 400°F/200°C.
2. Peel and trim the carrots, then cut in half lengthwise if they are small or into quarters if large.
3. Pound the coriander and cumin seeds in a mortar with a pestle, then blend in the chili, lemon juice, and oil.
4. In a large bowl, toss the carrots with the spice mix, then spread out on a nonstick baking sheet and roast in the oven for 20–25 minutes, or until the carrots are tender and golden brown.
5. Serve the carrots on a warmed plate with a good squeeze of lemon juice, garnished with fresh cilantro.

COOK'S TIP
• *This recipe works well with pumpkin and squash.*

Braised lentils with root vegetables, vinegar, and honey

Ⓥ | prep 20 minutes | cook 20–25 minutes | serves 4

1¾ oz (50 g), peeled weight, onion,
   diced
1¾ oz (50 g), peeled weight, carrot,
   diced
1¾ oz (50 g) celery, diced
1¾ oz (50 g), peeled weight, turnip,
   diced
1¾ oz (50 g) leek, diced
2 tbsp chopped fresh thyme
2 bay leaves
scant ½ cup dried Puy (French green)
   lentils
2½ cups vegetable stock
2 tbsp mature sherry vinegar
1 tbsp honey
black pepper

1. Heat a medium pan over high heat, add the vegetables, and cook for 2–3 minutes, stirring constantly, until golden brown.
2. Add the thyme, bay leaves, lentils, and stock and bring to a boil. Reduce the heat, cover, and let simmer for 15–20 minutes, or until the lentils are tender and have absorbed most of the stock.
3. Remove from the heat and stir in the vinegar and honey.
4. Serve on a warmed serving plate, with 1–2 grinds of black pepper.

COOK'S TIP
• *Serve these lentils with winter dishes such as casseroles, roasts, and braises, or as a vegetarian main meal.*

NUTRITION INFORMATION
per serving

calories	fat	sat fat
33	1 g	0.2 g

NUTRITION INFORMATION
per serving

calories	fat	sat fat
91	0.5 g	0.1 g

Being on a diet should not be restrictive. In fact, it is extremely important to eat as varied and as interesting a diet as possible. And if you normally enjoy eating desserts, there is no need to deprive yourself of this little pleasure in life.

Desserts

A whole range of delicious desserts can be created using interesting fruits, phyllo pastry, lowfat cream cheese, and yogurt. We can't promise you a sticky toffee pudding but try these wonderfully light recipes, which will satisfy any sweet tooth and provide a grand finale to any meal.

Steamed spiced exotic fruits

(V) | **prep** 20 minutes | **cook** 10–12 minutes | **serves** 4

2 kiwifruit, peeled and halved
4 rambutan or litchis, peeled, halved and pitted
2 passion fruit, the flesh scooped out
8 Cape gooseberries, papery leaves removed and fruit halved
3 oz (85 g), peeled weight, mango, cut into ¾-inch (2-cm) cubes
1 persimmon, cut into ¾-inch (2-cm) slices
⅜ cup fresh raspberries
2 vanilla beans, split in half lengthwise
2 cinnamon sticks, broken in half
4 star anise
4 fresh bay leaves
4 tbsp freshly squeezed orange juice

1. Preheat the oven to 400°F/200°C.
2. Cut four 16 x 16-inch (40 x 40-cm) squares of parchment paper and four foil squares of the same size. Put each parchment paper square on top of a foil square and fold diagonally in half to form a triangle. Open up.
3. Divide the fruits into 4 and arrange each portion in the center of each opened square—remember that you will be serving the fruit in the envelopes, so arrange the fruit neatly.
4. Add a vanilla bean half, a cinnamon stick half, a star anise, a bay leaf, and 1 tbsp orange juice to each triangle.
5. Close each triangle over the mixture, fold in the corners, and crumple the edges together to form airtight triangular bags.
6. Transfer the bags to a baking sheet and bake in the oven for 10–12 minutes, or until they puff up with steam.
7. To serve, put each bag on a serving plate and snip open at the table so that you can enjoy all the wonderful aromas as they are opened.

NUTRITION INFORMATION
per serving

calories	fat	sat fat
77	0.5 g	0.1 g

Banana and vanilla mousse cups

prep 20 minutes + 40 minutes chilling | **cook** 10 minutes | **serves** 4

scant 1 cup lowfat milk
1 vanilla bean, split in half lengthwise
½ tsp vanilla extract
1 tbsp cornstarch, blended with a little cold water
8¾ oz (240 g), peeled weight, banana, cut into ⅛-inch (3-mm) slices
1 tbsp superfine sugar
2 tbsp water
1 gelatin leaf, soaked in cold water
2 egg whites

for the decoration
¼ tsp unsweetened cocoa
4 fresh mint leaves

1. Pour the milk into a small pan and add the vanilla bean and extract. Bring to a boil. Gradually add the cornstarch mixture, stirring constantly, and cook until thickened. Remove from the heat and let cool.
2. Divide a third of the banana slices between four 9-fl oz (250-ml) glasses or cups.
3. Remove the vanilla bean from the thickened milk and add the remaining banana slices. Using a hand-held electric blender, blend the mixture until smooth, or use a food processor.
4. Put the sugar and water into a separate small pan and bring to a boil. Boil for 1½ minutes, then remove from the heat and stir in the soaked gelatin leaf.
5. In a large, very clean bowl, whisk the egg whites until soft peaks form, then whisk in the gelatin mixture. Using a metal spoon, gently fold in the banana mixture, being careful not to knock out the air in the whisked egg whites.
6. Pour the mixture over the sliced banana in the glasses or cups and place in the refrigerator to set for about 40 minutes.
7. To serve, lightly dust with unsweetened cocoa and decorate with mint.

COOK'S TIP
• *These cups can also be served lightly frozen on a hot summer's day. Just pop them into the freezer for 20–25 minutes before serving.*

NUTRITION INFORMATION
per serving

calories	fat	sat fat
100	1 g	0.6 g

Berry fruit cheesecake

prep 40 minutes + 1¹/₂ hours cooling/chilling | **cook** 15 minutes | **serves** 4

for the bases
⅛ cup oats
⅛ cup sunflower seeds
1 tbsp dried mixed berries
2 tbsp freshly squeezed orange juice

for the filling
1 tbsp water
2 gelatin leaves, soaked in cold water
1 tbsp honey
1⅛ cups cottage cheese
scant ½ cup 0% fat cream cheese
1 tbsp finely grated lemon zest
1 tbsp vanilla extract

for the topping
7 oz (200 g) frozen mixed summer fruits
1 tsp arrowroot, blended with a little cold water

1. Preheat the oven to 325°F/160°C.
2. To make the bases, put all the ingredients into a food processor and process to a paste. Spread out on a nonstick baking sheet and bake in the oven for 8 minutes. Remove, chop into ¹/₄-inch (5-mm) chunks, then return to the oven for an additional 4–5 minutes, or until golden brown. Let cool, then process again. The mixture becomes crisp when cold.
3. Divide the mixture between 4 mini gateaux rings or ramekins, pressing it into the bases.
4. To make the filling, put the water, gelatin leaves, and honey into a small pan over low heat and heat until the gelatin has dissolved.
5. Put the cottage cheese, cream cheese, lemon zest, and vanilla extract into a food processor and process for about 4–5 minutes, or until the mixture is really smooth and the zest has almost disappeared. Pour in the gelatin mixture—ensure that the cheese mixture is at room temperature before adding the gelatin, otherwise it will not set correctly.
6. Pour the filling over the top of the bases and let chill in the refrigerator for 30 minutes, or until set.
7. To make the topping, put the frozen fruit into a small pan over medium heat and bring to a boil. Gradually stir in the arrowroot mixture and cook, stirring constantly, until thickened. Let cool.
8. Add the topping to the cheesecakes. Using a small knife, carefully cut around the edge of each gateaux ring and tap out onto serving plates, or, if using ramekins, serve in the dishes.

NUTRITION INFORMATION

per serving

calories	fat	sat fat
130	2.5 g	0.7 g

Spiced baked goat yogurt with figs and maple syrup

(V) | **prep** 15 minutes | **cook** 15 minutes | **serves** 4

scant 1 cup goat yogurt
¼ tsp ground allspice
1 tsp maple syrup
¼ tsp vanilla extract
⅛ cup dried figs, very finely chopped
1 egg white

for the decoration
2 fresh figs, sliced
¼ tsp maple syrup
fresh mint leaves

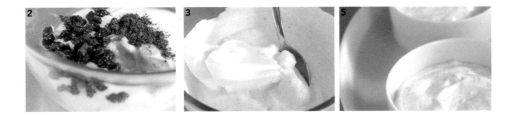

1. Preheat the oven to 275°F/140°C.
2. Mix the yogurt, allspice, maple syrup, vanilla extract, and dried figs together in a large bowl.
3. In a separate, very clean bowl, lightly whisk the egg white until soft peaks form. Using a metal spoon, fold into the yogurt mixture.
4. Spoon into 4 ramekins or a shallow, ovenproof dish.
5. Stand the ramekins or dish in a roasting pan and half-fill the pan with boiling water. Bake in the oven for 15 minutes or until set.
6. Remove from the oven. To serve, lay the fresh fig slices on top of the set yogurts, drizzle with maple syrup, and decorate with mint leaves.

COOK'S TIPS
• *These baked yogurts can be served with other fruits such as peaches or pears when in season.*
• *The yogurts can be served either hot or cold.*

NUTRITION INFORMATION

per serving

calories	fat	sat fat
60	2 g	1 g

Roasted European plums with honey, lavender, rosemary, and red currants

Ⓥ | prep 25 minutes | cook 20 minutes | serves 2

3 tbsp prune juice
2 tbsp freshly squeezed orange juice
4 strips of orange zest, cut with a potato peeler
1 sprig of rosemary
2 sprigs of lavender flowers, plus extra to decorate
1 tsp honey
⅛ cup red currants
9 oz (250 g) ripe European plums, halved and pitted
3 tbsp 0% fat plain yogurt, strained, to serve

1. Preheat the oven to 425°F/220°C.
2. Put the prune juice, orange juice and zest, rosemary, lavender, and honey into a small pan over low heat and let simmer for 4–5 minutes, until you have a light syrup. Remove from the heat, add the red currants and let cool.
3. Line a roasting pan with parchment paper and arrange the plum halves in it, cut-side up. Spoon half the syrup over the plums, then roast in the oven for 15 minutes until soft. Remove from the oven.
4. Arrange the plums on a serving plate, spoon over the remaining syrup, and top with the yogurt. Decorate with lavender before serving.

COOK'S TIPS
• *This dish can be served hot or cold but is best served warm with chilled yogurt.*
• *Choose only ripe plums for this dish so that the skins can be removed after roasting.*

NUTRITION INFORMATION

per serving

calories	fat	sat fat
85	0.2 g	0 g

Fresh raspberry and strawberry trifle

V | prep 20 minutes + 40 minutes cooling | cook 10 minutes | serves 2

1 tsp orange zest
generous ½ cup fresh strawberries
black pepper, to taste
½ tsp arrowroot
1 tsp Cointreau
5 tbsp freshly squeezed orange juice
6 tbsp buttermilk
½ tsp vanilla extract
1 tsp sugar
15 g (½ oz) cooked meringue, broken into ¼-inch (5-mm) pieces
⅜ cup fresh raspberries, plus extra to decorate
blanched strips of orange zest, to decorate

1. Mix the orange zest, strawberries, and 1–2 grinds of black pepper together in a bowl.
2. Blend the arrowroot with the Cointreau. Put the orange juice into a small pan over medium heat and bring to a boil. Gradually stir in the arrowroot mixture and cook, stirring constantly, until thickened. Remove from the heat, cover with plastic wrap to prevent a skin forming, and let cool completely.
3. Mix the buttermilk, vanilla extract, and sugar together in a separate bowl.
4. Divide the strawberry mixture between 2 glasses, then pour over the thickened orange juice. Sprinkle the crumbled meringue on the strawberries, top with the raspberries, and finally the vanilla buttermilk.
5. Decorate with a few extra raspberries and orange zest strips.

COOK'S TIP
• *These trifles are best arranged in the glass just before serving so that the meringue layer remains crunchy.*

NUTRITION INFORMATION

per serving

calories	fat	sat fat
105	0.5 g	0.2 g

Blueberry phyllo tart with lemon glaze

Ⓥ | **prep** 20 minutes + 40 minutes cooling | **cook** 15 minutes | **serves** 2

4 sheets of phyllo pastry
canola or vegetable oil spray
⅞ cup 0% fat cream cheese
1 tsp honey
1 tbsp finely grated lemon zest
3 tbsp lemon juice
1 tsp superfine sugar
scant ½ cup fresh blueberries

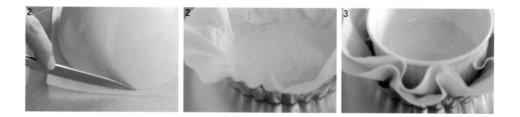

1. Preheat the oven to 350°F/180°C.
2. Using a plate as a guide, cut out four 5½-inch (14-cm) circles of phyllo pastry (you need two circles per tartlet). Spray each lightly with oil before laying two circles into two 4-inch (10-cm) fluted tartlet pans, pressing the pastry into the corners. Prick the bases with a fork.
3. Put a ramekin into the center of each tartlet shell to prevent the pastry rising, then bake in the oven for 5 minutes. Remove the ramekins and bake the shells for an additional 4–5 minutes so that the bases cook. Remove from the oven and leave the shells to cool in the pans. Store in an airtight container so that they remain crisp.
4. Mix the cream cheese with the honey in a small bowl.
5. Put the lemon zest, juice, and sugar in a small pan over low heat and heat until the liquid has evaporated, then add the blueberries. Stir with a metal spoon to coat the berries in the syrup. Remove from the heat and keep warm.
6. To serve, place each tartlet shell on a serving plate, spoon in a good dollop of the cream cheese mixture, then spoon over the warmed blueberries.

COOK'S TIPS
- *Make the tartlet shells in advance and keep for up to 3 days in an airtight container.*
- *The tartlets should be assembled just before serving so that the pastry does not become soggy.*

NUTRITION INFORMATION

per serving

calories	fat	sat fat
80	0.7 g	0 g

Really easy apricot and passion fruit sherbet with sesame snaps

(V) | **prep** 30 minutes + 2¹/2 hours freezing | **cook** 25 minutes | **serves** 6

for the sherbet
generous ½ cup no-soak dried apricots
generous 1 cup water
2 tbsp freshly squeezed lemon juice
2 tbsp freshly squeezed orange juice
3½ fl oz (100 ml) passion fruit pulp, strained to remove the seeds

for the sesame snaps (makes 16 snaps)
1 tbsp sesame seeds
1 tbsp liquid glucose
3 tbsp superfine sugar
2 tbsp all-purpose flour

1. To make the sherbet, put the apricots into a pan with the water and bring to a boil. Reduce the heat and let simmer for 10–15 minutes, or until the apricots are soft. Remove from the heat.
2. Using a hand-held electric blender or a food processor, purée the apricots with the water, then blend in the lemon juice, orange juice and 3 tbsp of the passion fruit pulp.
3. Add 2 tbsp of the passion fruit pulp, mix well, then transfer to a large, freezer-proof container and freeze for 20 minutes.
4. Beat the sherbet to break down the ice crystals, then return to the freezer. Freeze for an additional 2 hours 10 minutes, or until fully frozen, beating every 20 minutes to give a smooth texture to the finished sherbet.
5. To make the sesame snaps, preheat the oven to 350°F/180°C.
6. Heat a small pan over high heat, add the sesame seeds, and cook, tossing the pan, until golden brown. Remove from the heat, add the glucose, sugar, and flour and mix with a metal spoon to form a sticky paste. Remove from the pan and let cool slightly.
7. Roll the paste into a sausage shape and cut into 16 equal-size pieces.
8. With wet hands, roll each piece into a small round ball (add a little room temperature water if the paste is too dry), then lightly press out onto a sheet of silicone and bake in the oven for 6 minutes until golden brown. Remove from the oven. Using a palette knife, remove from the silicone and let cool on a wire rack, then transfer to an airtight container.
9. Using an ice-cream scoop, scoop the sherbet into glasses, spoon the remaining passion fruit pulp over the top, and serve with 2 sesame snaps per serving.

NUTRITION INFORMATION

per serving

calories	fat	sat fat
85	1.5 g	0.2 g

Index